Burn For You

CharlieDiana

Published by CharlieDiana, 2024.

While every precaution has been taken in the preparation of this book, the publisher assumes no responsibility for errors or omissions, or for damages resulting from the use of the information contained herein.

BURN FOR YOU

First edition. December 15, 2024.

Copyright © 2024 CharlieDiana.

ISBN: 979-8230406426

Written by CharlieDiana.

Table of Contents

Acknowledgment(s)

I want to give a special thanks to my mom, for always being there for me when I need her. For always supporting me, and for helping me. If she reads this, I want her to know how much I love and appreciate her. She's my best friend and mom wrapped up in one big sparkly bow.

I love you momma, and thank you for always being there when I need you.

Thank you to my friends and family who encouraged me to keep writing.

Chapter One

Willow

"Princess, it's time to get up." one of my maids, Lila, says as she opens the curtains to my room. Letting in all the sunlight, she ruins the rest of what remains of my peaceful slumber.

I groan as I rise from the bed. I'm sure I look like a rat, bedhead never suited my curly locks. I began to undress from my nightgown and waited for her to start dressing me. She approaches me with an ultramarine blue gown.

I wash my face in the wash bowl, patting dry, and she begins to put makeup on my face and pick out matching jewelry.

"Happy birthday Princess." she murmurs with a smile. "Thank you, Lila." I smile back. It's my birthday today.

I almost forgot about it. I was sleeping so well. "Have something extravagant laid out for me for tonight's celebration, it is my birthday after all." I laugh nervously.

She nods at me. After I slide my slippers on, I open my chamber door and greet the two guards stationed outside.

"You may escort me to breakfast." I say walking past the guards, smiling to myself. "Will my father be joining me this morning?" I ask the two muscle brains.

"Yes, Princess. He says he has an important discussion to talk to you about." The guard behind me, on my left, replies.

I nod in acknowledgement. Father always has important meetings to discuss, he hardly ever eats with me. Which I don't complain about. I learned my lesson on complaining a long time ago.

I once complained to my father about how I wanted to learn to ride a horse. I complained nonstop about it when I was younger, he grew tired of it. Eventually, he saw to it that the priest whipped my back with a six tailed whip in the throne room.

I now bear the scars on a hard lesson learned. I shudder at the memory. I clear my throat when we approach the doors to the dining hall. The two guards outside of it open the doors.

I nod at them. "Princess Willow of the Northern Kingdom!" one of the guards at the door yells, his voice echoing through the room. I keep my head held high as I walk to the table I see my father at.

Before sitting I give my father a courtesy bow and move to take my seat near him.

"Happy birthday Willow. Today is a big day for you." He says as he pours himself a chalice full of wine.

The burgundy liquid sloshing in it. "Is it?" I ask with a chuckle. Curiosity is my biggest flaw. It did kill the cat, maybe it won't get me. He nods with a swallow of his food and takes a sip from his chalice.

"Of course. After all, I am hosting a ball for your birthday, but not an ordinary ball. I am welcoming all our neighboring lords and kings. I have a deal for them to consider." He smiles wickedly at me.

The look in his eyes is almost deranged.

Dread sinks its cold claws in me. I resist the urge to shiver.

I furrow my brows questioningly. I eat my bacon as I wait for him to reply. "I am offering them your hand in marriage for a price. One hundred thousand gold shillings to be exact, and I expect you to listen and be compliant with whomever chooses you." I can feel my face drain of any color.

Why would he do this? I have worked hard to be the heir he wanted. Took all his beatings. I even allowed all his concubines to treat me like a foot soldier, even if their titles were below my own.

"If I may ask Father," I look at him waiting to see if his anger may rise at my words. When he simply nods I continue.

"Why now? I mean, I am not being a brash Father, I just wish to understand." I twiddle my thumbs waiting on the thunderous voice to come from him.

Instead he doesn't do anything.

"I am going to pretend you didn't ask that." He murmurs, continuing to drink his wine. I clear my throat and eat my food.

My eyes burn from blinking the sudden tears away.

Father left abruptly saying he had an important guest he was meeting and would be showing them around the castle today. I excused myself from breakfast and went towards the gardens.

It was the only place I could breathe in this stone prison which is my home.

My two guards trailing along behind me like lost puppies. When I make it outside the castle I stop and release the breath I hadn't realized I had been holding.

I hold my hand up to signal to the guards to wait here at the doors and walk toward the bench that sits in the center of the flower garden.

Surrounded by different types of flora and trees, it's my favorite place to read and relax.

The maids always make sure I have books outside to read.

It is the only way I am able to escape the harsh reality I live in.

It's the only activity Father didn't forbid. He thinks women should at least have a decent thing to do as a pastime activity when their husbands aren't around.

I turn my face up to the sun basking in its warmth, watching the clouds and feeling the wind.

I don't know how long I sat there doing nothing when I heard someone clear their throat.

I quickly stand and smooth out my dress.

I clasp my hands and turn to the stranger. My eyes widened. The man in front of me is gorgeous. His blue eyes are almost white, like crystal. His hair is white too.

Long but shaved in the back halfway down and tied up against his head. His skin is deeply tanned like he spends everyday in the sun. His body is god-like, I can see the muscles on his biceps strain against the sleeves he has rolled up.

When I realize I'm basically undressing this man with my eyes I struggle to bring them back to his face where he is now smirking.

Clearing my throat, "I apologize for my rudeness, I wasn't aware that anyone was out here." I smile as I twiddle my thumbs together.

He nods as he approaches me, "It's alright, I didn't realize this was someone's library or else I would have left you alone." he smiles with a nod of his head towards my books.

I chuckle and feel a blush creeping up my chest. "Yes, well it's better than being stuck inside a castle all day everyday. It's peaceful and quiet." I shrug.

He's closer to me now, and I swear I feel like the man is emitting heat waves.

I suddenly remember I never introduced myself nor did he.

"I forgot, pardon my rudeness again. My name is Willow. Princess of the Northern Kingdoms, and you are?" I asked while raising my brow. He chuckles to himself and shakes his head.

The sound sent a flustering heat straight to my abdomen. Holy hell this man can make me aroused just by making sounds.

"Well Princess," he bows, "I'm King Everest, King of the dragons." I raise both eyebrows at him this time, I'm sure shock is written across my face.

Suddenly I stutter, "O-oh my Lord, I'm terribly sorry for my disrespect-"

He puts a hand up, stopping me from rambling and I flinch.

Something passes over his features too quickly and I can't register it.

"No, it's alright. I enjoy being addressed like a regular person instead of a king. It feels nice for a change." He says while withdrawing his hand.

My face is burning now, I know I am as red as a cherry. His eyes are enthralling, truly gorgeous.

Lila's voice breaks me out of my trance, "Princess it's time to prepare for the ball!" Her voice carries around us and I step away from him.

"Well, it was a pleasure meeting you, your grace." I am curtsy with a smile.

He dips his head towards me and I turn and head towards the entrance to the castle, I feel his eyes burning into me with every step I make.

I turn around when I reach my guards, King Everest is gone, and a small smile forms on my face.

Chapter Two

Willow

THE WALK BACK TO MY chambers with Lila is filled with thoughts of the dragon king.

Lila helps me to undress and into the tub of hot water she drew for me. She helps me wash my body, careful not to wet my hair.

Lila is the only maid I have. She's the one who helped clean me up after my Fathers beatings and has always been there for me. She became my maid the day my mother died suddenly.

Thoughts of King Everest creep into my mind and I smile to myself. He really is breathtakingly gorgeous.

Helping out of the tub, Lila dries me and helps me put some scented lotion on. I always have to wear lotion due to my scars, if I don't they itch horribly.

Lila picked out a black and white gown.

The trim was white with black lace, from my breasts to the front of my mid area and the front of my legs, the lace pattern was the same.

The lace resembled many intricate patterns and swirls, some looked like leaves.

"This is beautiful Lila." I mumble in awe. She nods with a smile, "As always Princess."

She dresses me in the gown and I sit in front of the vanity she gets to work on jewelry and my makeup.

"Your father wanted me to make sure you remember what he said this morning." She says as she rubs blush on my cheeks.

I nod and fumble with my fingers. Of course he'd drag Lila into this.

There's a warning in there that if I fail or embarrass him, I'm sure I will have more scars to lather every night.

Once Lila was finished with my makeup she started pulling out jewelry.

She had chosen a black crown with black and clear diamonds to place on my head. She had decided to put my hair halfway up, leaving strands to frame my full face.

She put diamond earrings in my ear that dangle, touching my shoulder slightly when I move. And a black chain necklace.

Lila hummed in approval at her work, making me smile.

"Just one more thing." she whispered, grabbing some lipstick.

I pucker my lips as she rubs the stick on my lips. When she's done I roll my lips and finish with a pop.

I sigh and put my black heels on.

"Now, I have an entrance to make, dances to do, a Father to please, and to meet my future husband." I smile at her and she nods at me.

I start heading to the door when it opens abruptly, my Father entering my chambers.

"F-father, what a surprise. What's going on?" I ask. I can smell the whiskey from here.

His face is flush and he's stumbly. "I just wanted to make sure you were dressed appropriately for tonight, plus I am escorting you myself to the ballroom." He raises his tone with a hiccup, and I squinch my eyes.

"Of course Father. Shall we go then. I'm sure your guests are waiting patiently to meet you." I force a smile, trying to convince him to turn around.

He holds his arm out for me to loop mine through. I approach him slowly and do it.

He quickly turns and heads down the corridor. "You remember what I told you at breakfast. Don't disappoint me by having your head in the clouds girl." He growls and I nod my head.

Fear envelops me in its dark arms. When we approach the large grand doors to the ballroom, Father signals to the guards to open the doors and announce our arrival.

"Entering, His Majesty, The King of the Northern Kingdoms, King Raguel, and his daughter, Princess Willow, Princess of The Northern Kingdoms!" the guard behind us shouts and the ballroom is in an uproar of applause.

Father approaches the rail that overlooks the ballroom and waves to everyone below. I just smile and look pretty to marry.

Father leads me down the staircase on the side that meets the crowd below. He releases my arm and makes his way to his throne.

I look around and smile at the crowd. I'm searching for someone.

Someone who looks too good to be a king and who could possibly have more entertaining conversations. I grab a glass of wine from one of the scullery maids passing through, smiling at her.

I can't seem to locate him, so with my cup of wine in hand I sigh and head to stand beside my father.

"Now entering His Majesty, King Everest, King of The Dragons, ruler of Taegador Kingdom!" a loud voice from the overlook thunders through the room.

I'm on the steps that lead to my fathers throne when I look up and see Everest peering over the overlook.

He scans the crowd until his eyes land on me, I can feel the flush creeping up my chest. His lips twitch into a devilish grin.

I smile and look down and make my way to stand by my Father, Everest's eyes are burning my backside.

From where I am standing I can see everyone in the crowd. Sipping my wine I look over the rim and see the familiar white haired man.

He's talking with other men but more importantly there's a cackling hen party around him that seemed to flock together out of nowhere, all fanning their faces with hand held fans, some fanning their breasts.

Something twists inside my chest and I'm not sure what it is, when I bring my eyes back to Everest he's already looking at me.

A playful smile forms on his face when his eyes travel lower, taking in my dress.

He dismisses himself from his group and makes his way towards my father and I.

I immediately look elsewhere, feeling the blush burn my cheeks.

"Your Royal Highness, might I ask for your daughter's hand in a dance?" His rough yet smooth voice seems to caress every part of me. Father raises his hand with a nod and I grasp my gown, setting my wine on the table.

"Your Highness," I say as I give a small curtsy to Everest, he offers me his hand, and I take it. His hands are rough and calloused, his touch feels like it is searing into my skin.

Heat radiates off of him. He nods at a few men here and there while leading me to the center of the ballroom. I can tell by the other women who are frowning with heated cheeks that they have tried all evening to get him to dance just for him to ask for my hand.

I small smile tugs at my lips in joy that I'm his first. When we stop in the center I stand in front of him and bow, he bows as well.

He steps forward and takes one hand in his, and places the other at the small of my back. I in turn place my free hand onto his shoulder while looking up at him.

"What happened to just friendly chatting and no titles?" he asks as looks into my eyes.

His breath causes a shiver to run down my spine, my face burns at how close he is and my breath hitches.

"Is it not disrespectful to call you just by name in front of many onlookers?" I ask with a raised brow as we begin to side step in a circle. He hums to himself and I find myself looking at his lips.

"Are you enjoying the party Princess?" He asks, facing towards our next step.

I nod, "Of course, what girl doesn't like a party where she's just sold to the highest bidder." sarcasm and malice is evident in my tone.

I snap my lips closed with wide eyes and look at him.

His brows furrowed as looks at me. If father finds out I said anything, it'll be my skin he tans.

"Please, do not mention to my Father that I have said that." I whisper. No ordinary person would have heard me but he's a dragon, of course he heard it.

He nods at me, his eyes searching mine. "You, Princess, are the most gorgeous woman in this room. Anyone should be honored to just even breathe the same air as you. I would be overjoyed to have you in my court everyday." He says with a smile.

I smile at him and ask, "What is your kingdom like?" Mother told me when I was younger what the kingdom of dragons was like, but I wanted to hear it from the king of dragons.

"It's gorgeous. It's an open concept and much larger than this castle. Most of the balconies have large landings and entry ways for a dragon to fit through, every room has one. You can see the sunsets and sunrises everyday from my balcony. Dragons are always flying through the sky." when he talks there's a twinkle in his eye that tells me how much he loves his kingdom.

"I, um, I have never seen a dragon. Well, I have met you, but I mean I haven't seen any scales or tails." I laugh.

He chuckles with me, as he spins me under his arm and back to his chest. "Well Princess, if you ask nicely I may show you my dragon one day. Although I will forewarn you, he is a menace. He enjoys being overly persistent, dominant, he always gets what he wants."

The fire in his eyes gets darker and the heat radiates off of him in waves. I catch my breath as I look from his eyes to his lips.

That familiar heat and pain shoot to my abdomen. "I would love to see your dragon and your kingdom, Everest." I say his name like it's my last breath.

A rumbling sound comes from his chest. "Of course, Princess. Now do you trust me, enough to lead this dance to the finish?" he asks.

Of course I trust him, I'm not sure why but I feel like if my life depended on him I could always rely on him. I nod with a smile.

"Good now hold onto my shoulders." he whispers. I move my hand from his and grasp his shoulders.

The muscles underneath flex at my touch. His hands grab my waist, and next thing I know he's lifting me like I weigh a feather. And then we begin to spin in intricate circles. I look down and his eyes are on mine with a smirk tugging his lips upward.

I smile back at him. This time though the smile reaches up my face, a genuine smile.

Chapter Three

Everest

WHEN I FIRST LAID EYES on her, I expected her to just willingly throw herself for me to have. Instead, she didn't even know who I was.

Her eyes were gorgeous, and the way she kept getting flustered, her breath always catching. When she left to get ready for the ball I had to adjust myself in my trousers.

My dragon wanted her just as much as I did.

Setting her back down onto the ballroom floor, after spinning her she's glowing with joy. I reach out and tuck a strand of hair behind her ear, surprised at how soft it is.

I grab her hand and press my lips to it with a bow. "I will show you sometime Princess, for now I have some business to attend to with your Father. Goodnight Princess." I smile as I turn to leave.

I smell the arousal and disappointment coming from her. Her father has an opposition for me and some of the other lords here. I make my way to the door that leads to the King's private office.

Some of the other men followed me.

The door opens and I make my way to sit in a seat across from his desk.

"I'm glad to see you all made it." Raguel praises, his cheeks are rosy and the stench of whiskey and wine rushes from him.

"Tell us Your Highness, what is this grand ball for?" another man asks.

The King laughs as he sits in his chair. "Well, as you all know my daughter has turned eighteen today, this is her birthday ball. But, I am putting her on the marriage market. For a price of course. I know my daughter's beauty is closer to the gods than those creatures out there. She's been trained well, at my and the priest's hand. All I am asking is for one hundred thousand gold shillings." he looks at each of us.

Now, what she had said about being sold makes sense. I doubt she can object to her father.

I growl and rise from my seat, placing my hands on the desk, "So you'll just sell your flesh and blood, the heir to your throne, to some idiot with a cock, for what?"

My voice cuts through everyone in the room, causing most to flinch but not the king, he just smiles.

"A woman doesn't deserve to sit on the throne, they don't think rationally. They think with their heart, you have to have a brain to sit on the throne. But I forget you dragons have different ideals and morals." He sneers.

"That's a high price just for some piece of ass to have by our side." A man behind me says and another growl erupts from my throat.

Why would a father want to sell his only heir, unless she isn't the only one and she doesn't know about it. My dragon paces inside me at this man's audacity to sell his own.

She's a wonderful girl, a sweet girl. I doubt he was involved in her life very much, I know her mom died from an illness when she was a child, or that's what everyone had said. "What's in it for you besides the money?" I ask.

He drinks wine from his chalice and swishes it around before swallowing with a smack of his lips, "I get to make room, like I said women shouldn't be on the throne. One of my mistresses is pregnant, and we had a shaman confirm the gender is a boy. He'll be my heir, the next to rule the kingdom."

There it is, that's the hand he wants to deal with. He wants to make room so no other child can fight his son for the title.

"Where should I have the money sent?" my words are rushed and there is this crawling feeling in my heart, my dragon is itching to fly.

He's furious that someone who calls himself a father is willing to throw their only and oldest daughter away like rubbish.

He looks bewildered at a moment, I can hear everyone's rushing heartbeats.

Then he laughs, causing me to furrow my brows. "You, a dragon, are willing to pay for my daughter? To hand over your gold just for a girl?" He states, his jolly green stomach bouncing with his laughter.

In one swift motion I'm over his desk, my hand wrapped around his throat, and his back up against the wall.

"I asked you a question, Your *Highness*, let's not forget who has the upper hand and can burn this whole damn castle to the ground." I growl, I allow my dragon to seep through my eyes, welcoming his presence.

The king squirms in my grasp, "Y-you can give it to my steward, I expect it soon." he gasps for breath when I let him go. I fix the sleeves of my shirt up to my biceps.

"Let this be known, I King Everest of The Dragons, take Princess Willow to be my mate and rule by my side as Queen of The Dragons. Not just some piece of tail at my side." I give a pointed look to the pale King who is rubbing his neck.

Without a sudden word, I leave his office and go to my temporary chambers. I'm walking through the crowd of the ballroom when I catch her scent.

Wildfire smoke, hibiscus, and worry.

I come to a stop, and find her worried gaze on me, I give her a reassuring smile before leaving the room.

Rushing into my chamber doors, I start unbuttoning my shirt. Drake cat calls from his perch on a chaise sofa in the corner of a room.

"Well, what did the King do to get you in a twist, brother?" he smirks, Drake, my second in command, my ally, assassin and personal guard, has always been able to read me.

I sigh and begin to pour myself a chalice of whiskey.

"He's selling his daughter." I murmur taking a sip.

Drake hums to himself, "Well who bought her?" he asks.

My shoulders tense and I turn to his gaze. "I made an irrational decision, caught in the moment." Drake raises his brows slowly and nods.

"There is never anything irrational about you Ev. You did what you thought was right, what else happened?" he clasps his hands together on his lap.

I sigh and rub my temple, "I perhaps have made an announcement before the King and other lords that I will take her as my mate and she will rule beside me as Queen of The Dragons. I can not deny that I want her and so does my dragon. She's soft, sweet, and smells devine to us."

Drake just shrugs with a smile and I groan, "Drake, I don't even know how humans really work. Their morals or beliefs, it's completely different from ours. How am I supposed to do this?" I raise my shoulder and use my hands to motion around.

"Well, how much money do I need to send to his Royal High-ass? And second, you said you wanted her, but does she want you?" Drake asks, shrugging one shoulder with his head tilted, he's got a curious humor behind his eyes.

I place my hands on my hips and pace. "She said she wanted to see my dragon, and my kingdom. She smiles brightly when I'm around, and she's always flustered too. She's different, she also doesn't sit around with other ladies and whisper while eyeing me and fanning their tits. And take that prick a large chest, tell him that she isn't to be touched or disrespected, she's mine." I point at the ground with a growl.

She isn't like them at all. I also feel like she's adventurous and curious.

Drake nods and heads to the door, and stops abruptly.

The sudden scent of hibiscus, wildfire smoke, and shock invade my nostrils. I lounge forward and push Drake to the side, tearing the door open.

"Princess." I breathe.

Her wide eyes travel from my face down my chest, abs, and to the v line that stands out.

A bright red flush spreads from her neck to her cheeks. There's pain and a welling of tears in her eyes. Her eyes snap up to mine,

"Y-you bought me. From my F-father?" she asks with a pain in her voice and I wince internally at myself.

"She must have heard us through the doors." Drake says in my mind. "It's not like that Princess. I meant you no harm." I plead.

I go to reach for her but she flinches back and shakes her head before she turns and runs down the hallway. "Shit." I curse myself and run my hand through my hair.

Reaching out with my hearing I tried to find the sound of her breathing and heartbeat to see where she's going.

"Drake, go take care of the King." I say with my eyes closed and I hear him close the door behind himself.

Still trying to listen, I found her. She's heading to the gardens. I know now isn't the perfect time I wanted her to see my dragon, but he'll reach her quicker.

With a groan I begin to undress. There isn't enough room for me to shift in here, so I will have to jump out of the window. Opening the shutters, I look down, nobody but guards are patrolling.

The gardens are on the other side of the castle.

I blow a breath and jump, allowing the dragon to take over. My first shift hurt all those centuries ago, but now it's just as simple as flicking a bug.

I can feel all my bones shifting and growing, some snapping to form other bones. When I open my eyes I also unfurl my wings, allowing the wind to carry me.

I shake my head and neck, relieving the tension. I turn and fly with a curve alongside the castle until the gardens come into view.

Just as I'm approaching I see her sitting in an open area, her knees tugged to her chest and her forehead resting on the tops of her knees.

I slowly furrow my wings to allow me to decline from the sky. Unfurrowing them to flap a little as I land. I watch as the sudden gusts of wind from my wings disturbs her hair until she raises her head and sees me.

Her eyes are wide, red rimmed and puffy from crying. I don't approach, allowing her to look. I'm too afraid that I'm going to scare her away.

"Do not cry Princess. I didn't mean to scare you, I apologize. I understand you would like an explanation of what you heard, yes?" I reach out to her with my voice from the dragon.

She nods but still examines me with her eyes. *"Your father was offering your hand in marriage, or anything really, to every lord in that ball tonight. Even to the ones who just referred to you as a prize or trophy."*

"So, I gave him the gold he wanted for you. I'm not trying to make it seem like I'm forcing you, I would never hurt you Willow. I didn't want those other men to get you and force a life you would not want."

"I'm sorry it seemed that way. I didn't mention it to you before because I needed time to think. You can tell me right now that you want me to leave you alone and I will. I'll have a house built for you inside my kingdom and I will leave you alone." I say while shifting so I can sit.

She stands up, still sniffling. "You could have told me. I'm not a child. I know how to have an adult conversation, Everest. Instead I found out by accidentally hearing it." She waves a hand and uses her other to wipe her eyes.

"I don't know what you will expect of me since you bought me. I have never been with a man. I'm not experienced. You're a man who has more experience with this stuff than I do. I'm sorry to disappoint you, but you would have better luck with a woman who actually knows what she's doing." She half smiles and raises her arms.

I shake my head, growling. I say, *"Willow, I don't just go around sleeping with women. I also didn't buy you to just fuck you."*

Her brows furrowed and her eyes were glistening.

A familiar blush turns her cheeks red. She walks up to me and points at my snout, "Then what do *you* want with me, King Everest?" She's angry at me.

She is upset I kept her in the dark. Gods, she's even more gorgeous when she's angry, she's feisty, and it's a huge turn on.

"Willow, that's enough alright, let's talk more in the morning when we've calmed down." I murmur.

She shakes her head and places a defiant foot down. I sigh, *"Princess, just please come back into the castle with me and we will talk about it in the morning, I promise. After tomorrow, if you would like to come with me to my kingdom you can."*

She raises her head and looks me in the eye. It takes a moment of silence until she nods and starts to walk back to the castle. Drake is already by the door, my clothes in his hand.

He says something to her low enough I can't hear and a possessive growl erupts through me. Drake raises his hand in peace and I quiet down.

He hands her the clothes before he turns and leaves. Willow begins to walk back to me, her tears are dried now.

"I'm going to set these right here so you can shift back and get dressed. But know this Everest, you can't hide things from me if you want me to marry you." she murmurs while setting my clothes on the ground.

I wait for her to have her back facing me before I shift. I grab my clothes and turn my back to her as well and begin to pull my trousers on.

I know she turned and peeked a look when I heard her breath hitch and heartbeat increase.

Her arousal invades my nose when I take a deep breath. I stifled a groan from the pain in my balls, this girl doesn't even have to try to get me hard.

Just being near her does the trick. I turn to face her while pulling my shirt on only to find her staring right at me. Her face is flustered and her breathing is erratic, she's undoubtedly turned on by me as well.

I raise a brow and smirk, "See something you like, Princess?" I ask. Her face turns a deeper shade and she turns around too fast and loses her footing. I reach my arms out and grab her, but not until I too fall with her.

I use one arm to keep us from hitting the ground and another wrapped around her waist.

Gently I lay her on her back on the soft dewy grass. "You may want to refrain from moving fast Princess, also I wasn't sure how to talk to you about it." I murmur in her ear and watch her thundering pulse in her neck.

I go to stand up but she wraps her arms around my neck and pulls me back down towards her. My face is inches from hers as she speaks, "I mean it when I say I have zero experience." Her voice is soft and trembling.

I smile at her "Princess, I wont do anything to you unless you want me to, is that clear? Do you want to go inside now?" I ask.

She looks at my lips then back to my eyes before shaking her head. I raise an inquisitive brow at her, "What do you want then, Princess?" She shrugs, seeming to shrink in on herself, "I-I don't know what I want."

"Well, when you know, you let me know, okay?" I say as I rub my thumb across her cheekbone and she nods.

Chapter Four

Willow

Lila's helping me pack my things from my chamber and humming to herself. Last night I had wanted to kiss Everest so badly but I was also angry with him.

When I saw his naked back I couldn't stop myself from taking a peak lower. When he asked if I saw something I liked, I did

"Princess, I was made aware that I would be going with you to Taegador Kingdom, would it be alright if I placed my things with yours?" Lila asked.

I smiled at her, "Of course Lila. We'll probably save room that way too." We continued to gather my things when a knock came from my door.

"Come in!" I yell. When I turn around I'm greeted by a freshly bathed Everest with wet hair.

Sudden memories of last night come to mind and I turn back around to keep myself busy.

"I see you are packing your things, which means you'll be joining me in my kingdom?" he asks, looking around my chambers.

I nod, "If you bought me that means you know how worthless I am to my father, and I'm pretty certain being in your kingdom will be better than here." It had to be true, anywhere would be better than living under my father's thumb always at his beck and call.

I shudder when I feel his eyes travel down my body. I'm wearing a simple burgundy dress with my hair up. I chose not to wear any makeup or jewelry.

My hair being up shows off my collar bones that I've always gotten compliments about.

"We'll take a carriage to my kingdom so we can carry everything and since I'm pretty sure neither of you will be comfortable flying on our backs. It will also give me time to explain how my kingdom works. We will leave at noon." he says as he clasps his hands behind his back.

I watch him from the corner of my eye as I'm holding two dresses up picking between the two.

He turns to leave but stops and puts his hand on the wall, "Pick the blue one Princess." Then he leaves.

I blush when I realize I'm holding a very intimate looking dress. It's an off the shoulder day gown, it has a slit in the front that shows the inside of my breasts but not too much.

I hand it to Lila to put into the chest with my other dresses.

I dismissed Lila when we were finished so she could get herself ready, she had sent tea and cookies up to my chamber so I could snack and read before we left.

My door bursting open and almost breaking the hinges made me spill the hot tea I was holding on to my hands, scalding them.

I winced and looked up, ready to demand an answer when I saw it was my Father.

"F-father what's going on?" I asked, raising from my seat, still holding my hands where they were now burned. "You fucking whore." He seethed.

I stood there wide eyed instead of being smart and running from his now blooming wrath.

"So, what did you do, hm? Did you spread your legs to him and make him choose you?" I flinched at his words.

"W-what? N-no Father, I'm still a virgin." I plead. He is the one who sold me, why would he be upset?

The last thing I see before finding myself on the stone floor is his hand coming toward my face. The side of my face burns and hurts, I taste blood in my mouth.

"Father, stop please!" I plead. The tears burned my eyes, causing everything to be blurry.

"You fucking whore!" He shouts as he kicks me in the ribs.

My body flies into the stone flooring, banging my head on the cool floor. I cry out and then there's a crashing sound nearby and what sounds like gurgling.

A Loud possessive growl erupts. And I try so hard to blink away the pain and tears.

Before me, in my room, Everest has my father pinned by his throat up against a wall.

"I thought I made myself clear, Raguel, you do not touch what is mine! Instead, you come into her room, you beat her and disrespect her while knowing she's under my protection as she is soon to be my Queen?!" his voice thunders, the dragon in him dangerously close to coming to the surface.

I watch as he grabs my fathers wrist, "For her wounds require a price." Then he snaps it like a twig and my father begins to scream in agony.

"E-Everest, please." I whimper. He immediately lets my father fall to the floor and rushes over to me.

His eyes now have gold specks in them from his dragon. He picks me up off the floor. I sob, grabbing his shirt ignoring the searing pain in my hands.

"Shh baby, I've got you now." he coos as he picks me out of the floor. We're walking now but I don't know where we are going, my body continues to rack with sobs and pain.

I feel Everest lay me down on something and pull my body flush against his. He pets the back of my head while whispering sweet nothings in my ear. When I can't cry anymore and just sniffle he nuzzles into my hair.

I looked around where we were, and noticed we were in his temporary chambers on his bed, I blush.

His bed smells like him, like forests and something wild and untamed, "Tell me where you are hurting and let me fix it?" he asks.

I nod, "My face and head, also my ribs. My hands are scalded from the tea I was drinking." I murmur. He hums and grabs my two hands in his large one.

"This is going to feel cold at first, but it should feel better after a second." he says just as his hands turn from searing heat to frigid coolness.

I wince from the feeling and the sound that escapes my mouth doesn't even sound like me.

When he pulls away I find his hand on my face, I lean into it, accepting the coolness.

Another moan.

His breath hitches as he watches me and my face burns.

Looking away from me, he clears his throat, "Turn over Willow."

I nod my head just an inch and face the other way, my back towards him. He repositions himself where he can see my whole back.

I feel his hands move up my back.

He starts to untie my corset, pulling the strings. Then his hand finds the nape of my neck where the dress ties together.

His fingers skim my skin and I shiver. He pulls the strings loose and I know he sees my scars by the way he growls.

"I'm sorry he did this to you, Princess." he murmurs. I shrug a shoulder, causing the dress to drift down my arm but not revealing my breasts.

His hand rubs up from my lower back to my shoulder then further inside my dress where his hand rests on my ribs.

The coldness returns and I grip the sheets and bury my face in them. The moan that escapes me sounds too wild. I feel myself getting wet and rubbing my thighs together.

He curses under his breath and in one swift motion he's above me, his thighs between my own. His gold flecks in his eyes still tell me his dragon hasn't subsided.

"Everest." I breathe his name like it's my last breath.

"Yes Princess?" he questions.

I look at his lips then back to his eyes. "Kiss me." I wasn't sure I had said it because he didn't move, until his lips were crashing into mine.

His lips are soft, but strong and dominant. Demanding.

His hands cup my face and I feel just how turned on he is against me. Moaning into his mouth from the friction.

The opening gives his tongue the chance it needs to sweep into my mouth.

His hand moves to grab my breast, squeezing and rubbing my nipple.

His kisses lead down my neck where he sucks, licks, and bites my skin. He growls against my skin, the vibration from it travels straight to my needy clit.

He pulls back and drags the shoulders of my dress down, taking a moment to look at my breasts. "You are beautiful, Princess." he whispers.

My face grows hot, "Even with the scars?" I ask. I've always been scared my scars would scare someone away.

"Your scars are a part of you, even if your whole body was scarred it wouldn't change who you are as a person. You're caring, kind, brave enough to yell and stomp your pretty little feet at a dragon king, and you don't judge anyone, that is what makes you beautiful, Princess." he's looming over my face when he says, then his mouth is on mine again.

He pinches and twists my nipple which earns him several moans and mewls.

"Tell me Princess, do you want to cum?" he asked, grabbing my hip and pulling me towards his erection.

God yes I would love to at this moment, with him. "I'm a virgin Everest." I whispered.

"I'm not taking your virginity here Princess. I'm just going to help you relieve that ache between your legs." he rubbed his erection between my legs, I arched my back into him, craving more from him.

I nod at him. He smiled and growled at the same time and I swear I have never heard anything more beautifully crafted.

I bite down on my bottom lip only for him to pull it out from my teeth and say, "These are mine to bite Princess, and these," he grabbed my breast again, "are mine to suck and play with and your pussy is mine to taste." he growls.

I sucked in a breath like it was my last. His words only made the ache worse and I groaned. "Everest, please." I begged.

He smiled and pinched my nipple, combining both pain and pleasure, "That's it Princess, beg for it." Lord if this man doesn't hurry I'm going to burst with need and want.

"Everest, please let me cum." I whimpered as I arched into him more, craving his touch. "As you command Princess." He inclined his head and grabbed my dress in bunches at my thighs raising them to meet my stomach.

He moved my shift out of the way and looked at my bare self before him. That familiar heat returned to my face as I watched him lick his lips.

He brings his face closer, I swear I heard him sniff me.

"You are exquisite Princess, and I'm going to taste you as you come on my face." he said as he looked into my eyes. His tongue darted out and flicked my clit.

"Oh" I moaned. His tongue slid from the entrance and back up to my clit. Then his whole mouth was on me.

His tongue sliding up and down, teasing my clit. I arched my back as I raised and propped on an elbow to watch, my other hand going into his hair.

His arms were under my thighs, his hands holding my legs apart for him.

The sounds with my uneven breathing don't sound like me, and it embarasses me.

He began to suck and bite my clit using his tongue to rub while he sucked. I was getting closer to the edge.

"Everest!" I arched my back, my head laying back down onto the soft pillows. My limbs and toes started tingling.

My thighs started to quiver and attempt to close on their own but he held them in place. My breath was ragged and my moans were frantic. He repeated his torture with his tongue suck, lick, bite.

The sounds were echoing around us.

"Oh Everest, I'm-" coming. I fisted his hair as I laid back and my body shook with an orgasm. The euphoric pleasure consuming me.

"That's it Princess. Let it go." Everest growled as he crawled up my body. He let me ride out the waves of bliss before he claimed my lips.

His tongue teasing my lips to open. I could smell myself on his face.

Opening my mouth, I let his tongue in, allowing his tongue to dominate my own. Tasting myself on him, I moaned in his mouth. My toes and legs were still tingling and my thighs were quivering.

My body felt exhausted yet fulfilled at the same time.

I knew sleep would try and take me soon, but I also knew we would leave in a few hours. Everest pulled me to his chest and I buried my face in his shirt.

He smelled devine, and welcoming yet dangerous underneath it all.

He combed his fingers through my hair, "You taste like everything I could have ever wanted." he murmurs.

I don't reply, suddenly self aware of what just happened between us.

"I can hear your heartbeat Willow, calm down. There is no need to be shy anymore." he chuckles, amused at me. I nod but don't dare to meet his eye.

"When we are at my home, I do not expect you to follow my rules or our customs and beliefs. But a few older dragons that make up my council will."

"They will expect that since I have now taken your hand, that you will obey me and do as you are told. I will never force you to do such a thing. My sister will be happy to have another royal female to dress with."

"But, a lot of dragons may not agree with my decision to take your hand, so I promise I will protect you there. They will grow to love you. You will be their Queen afterall." he smiled at me.

I took this moment to study his features.

He only had one dimple, which was on his left cheek. His eyes had creases from years of laughter. His promise of protecting me made me feel like I was noticed, my only hope was that he kept his promise to protect me.

I would need protection where we were going. The dragon kingdom isn't built for the weak, truly, only the strong survive there.

I give him a small smile.

"Now, we should probably meet everyone else and discuss which path we're going to take back to my kingdom, and should also make sure everything is prepared and ready to go." He whispers with a devilish smile while getting up.

A dark lustrous promise hiding beneath his words.

I chuckle and shake my head at him. He offers me a hand and helps me up from the bed.

He pulls me to his body quickly, "As my wife and mate also the soon-to-be Queen of my *entire* kingdom, I want you to know that you will always be my equal. If there is something that we do not agree on in the future we will talk about it and come to an agreement about it. I never want you to feel as if your opinion is not validated or is not needed." he lifts my chin with his finger so my gaze meets his eyes.

"Of course, nor yours, King Everest." I nod. His brows furrowed and his eyes moved from side to side, glancing into each of mine, like he was thinking extremely hard.

Similar to a drunken soldier trying to choose between more alcohol or more broads. He clears his throat, lord this man can get me off with just sounds.

"Also, Willow, you only call me by my name. I like the way it sounds out of your mouth. Especially," he gives a light squeeze with his other hand on my hip, and he brings his mouth to the shell of my ear. His breath tickled it, "when you're gasping for air when I'm making you unravel beneath my tongue."

His voice is raspy and I know he's thinking about what happened earlier, I don't blame him. It was otherworldly. My heart is beating wildly in my chest, I know he can hear it.

"We should hurry before someone comes to look for us." I whisper. Disappointed in myself, I should be all over him right now until I can't anymore.

He hums to himself. When he pulls away, his eyes are burning with want and lust. I can see an internal war behind his crystal-like eyes.

He tucks an arm behind his back while holding my hand with the other. I stay beside him as he opens the door and begins to lead me down the hallway.

A few servants and scullery maids nod or bow, acknowledging us as we pass them. A few lords and ladies even poke their heads from their chambers to see us walk, which is actually weird to me.

"Why are they watching us like owls waiting on a mouse to show?" I whisper to Everest. He chuckles and shakes his head.

"What is it?" I ask. What could be funny and why is everyone peeking out of their rooms to look at us?

"Let's just say that you, Princess, are not at all a quiet person." He glances over at me with a raised brow.

What in the actual- "Oh my gods!" I shriek with a whisper and cover my face with my other hand that isn't holding Everest's own.

Everest, then, has the audacity to roar a thunderous laugh, the sound echoing through the hallways. I'm sure anyone can hear it in the castle.

"Everest, it is not funny, stop before literally *everyone* comes to look at me." I growl at him.

"Why would I do that Princess? Your face is as red as a beet, not to mention your little anger spurt is making it worse. I love it when you get all shy, it's adorable. Besides, you, my dear, have nothing to worry about. No one will dare say anything to you in my presence, and soon even when I'm not around they wouldn't dare." He teases me, there is pure joy written on his face at my self-effacing.

It doesn't take long to reach the library where we are meeting Everests' companions. When we enter the room, there are 3 sets of heads. One I recognize is Lila. I give her a small smile which she returns.

The other two are men, one I recognize is the one who was with Everest the night I heard he bought me. The two men turn and bow their heads at Everest and I.

"Princess, these two men are Drake and Winslow. Drake is my 2nd. He takes care of things within my kingdom that I can't. Winslow here is one of the oldest living dragons in my kingdom. He's a member of the council." Everest speaks with a level tone, giving my hand a reassuring squeeze.

I nod my head in greetings to them. Drake is dark haired with green eyes, his sharp jaw is chiseled with a shadow of unshaven hairs.

His eyes have a playfulness in them. He's an impressive height, almost as tall as Everest is. He is also as built as Everest too.

Winslow is built and defined as well, his cinnamon colored hair has some grey floating around here and there. His gaze is stony and stark. He appears to be someone I don't want to be alone with, ever.

Everest lets go of my hand and approaches the men. He shakes hands with Winslow and hugs Drake.

The two must be close together. I stay rooted in the spot, Lila approaches and stands at my side.

"If everything is packed in the carriages we can go ahead and discuss which routes will be taken back to Taegador." Everest's voice echoes as he clasps both hands behind his back, looking down at the map splayed out on the lavish oak table.

Drake goes to stand beside him and points to somewhere on the map. "We can take the main road here, then head towards the Vargas Forest. We can get food and supplies we'll need there as well, seeing as that village is fine trading with us dragons for the right price." He says while his finger roams the map.

"I agree. Not to mention there will also be an inn for the Princess and her lady to sleep as well. From there we can go down to the village by the sea, Salas Village. They won't allow us to stay for long so we'd have to make camp outside of their borders." Winslow adds, rubbing a finger along his chin.

Salas Village is not keen on outsiders, they prefer to stay to themselves and hardly trade anything with anybody.

The village in Vargas Forest is full of easy-going people that just love money, but they also hate violence.

The one village in particular that even I knew we should avoid at all costs is Makeles Village. They despised dragons and despised royalty worse.

I've read stories of all the villages and even looked at a few maps when I was younger. I wanted to see the world, I wanted more to explore.

Drake and Everest both nod at Winslow's add-in. I'm not sure yet if this dragon is a friend or foe to me.

"Princess, what do you think?" Winslow asked, putting me in the spotlight all of a sudden causing my cheeks to set ablaze.

I cleared my throat and approached the table, studying the map and noting our route.

"As long as we avoid the Makeles Village, here," I pointed at the small town on the map, "then we should be all good. That village is not friendly to any of us here." When I looked up I saw Everest beaming at me with content, Winslow studying me a bit too close for my comfort, and Drake was watching it all unfold with humor.

"Well, I guess we have our route marked and we can head out of this damned castle now. This place is a bit too human-y for me." Drake sighed wistfully.

Chapter Five

Everest

I couldn't explain how proud I was when she proved she wasn't as dull as most Princesses. She knew exactly which village we should avoid at all costs.

I could feel Winslow's curiosity grow by the minute. Winslow wasn't a dragon we had to worry about. I already knew that he would test her somehow, I just didn't know when, and I wasn't expecting him to do it then.

Winslow has been around for ages, he used to be my grandfathers' 2nd before he died alongside his mate.

The dragon we'd have to worry about is currently visiting her homeland. Zephyra. The wench has had her talons out for me and the title of Queen since I reached maturity.

I could always smell deceit coming from her like the stench of death. When she returns, I'd have to be sure someone will always be with Willow until her coronation and our mating ceremony.

I will also have Drake start teaching Willow how to defend herself from one of the oldest creatures on this planet. When we return to my castle, I plan on taking Willow to my personal library.

Since she loves to read, I already see it is how she plans on spending her free time. My personal library holds more about the beginning of time than the regular library in the castle.

The scrolls and other documents are entrusted to the leaders of my kingdom for safeguarding, if they were to wind up in the wrong hands, it could spell out our extinction.

Too much information lies in my hands.

"Is everything alright Everest?" Willow asks, walking beside me toward the carriage. I nod, "Of course. I was just lost in thought there for a moment. Do not fret." I reassure her.

I will probably have to do that quite often when Zephyra shows her scaly ass. The dragon inside me bristles at the thought of that woman. I don't mind reassuring my mate.

I'm hers, since the moment she caught my attention in the garden.

She will always have me wrapped around her sweet little fingers. She will never have to long for anything, all she has to do is ask me for anything and I will have it done or retrieved for her.

I turn to Willow just before opening the carriage door. I looked around, not a single soul came to see her off. Which doesn't surprise me.

"When we arrive in Taegador Kingdom, there is a place in my castle I want to show you. It's a surprise though. It belongs to both of us now." I smile at her.

Just imagining her surprised smile and joyful delight has my dragon purring. She half cocks a smile with a raised eyebrow, intrigue etched on her face.

"How big of a surprise are you talking about?" She asks giggling.

I shrug and open the carriage door, holding out a hand, "Very big." This is the only detail I give her, helping her up and into the carriage.

I climb in after her, closing the door I pat the top of the carriage signaling the driver that we are ready to depart.

I position myself across from Willow. My tall stature barely manages to sit comfortably here. I stretch my right leg out, the outside of Willow's calf now close to my own.

Crossing my arms I look at her. She's looking out of the window, her small hand holding the curtain open. She rolls her lips together.

She's most likely trying to see if anyone is watching us out of the castle windows.

"What kind of books do you like to read?" I ask, attempting to distract her from her wandering thoughts.

"Well, I like to read about history and of course romance." She looks down and a small pink tint highlights her cheeks.

I smile, I love how easily she gets shy and tucks herself away. It makes me want to protect her from this cruel world even more.

"Well then, I'm sure you'll love the library at my castle." I smile at her. Her own smile beams back at me.

"I meant to tell you that Winslow is not one of the ones we have to worry about. He's curious about you, hence why he asked you that question earlier, you surprised him. The main one we have to worry about, her name is Zephyra. She's the oldest living female dragon in Taegador." I sigh and watch her expression.

Her face is blank, a great poker face. But her eyes say there is curiosity and a bit of jealousy.

So my little princess does get jealous? "No, Princess, I have never slept with her. She wants the title of queen and me on her arm. I've always known what she has wanted. Yes, I have slept with other women, but not her. So don't worry about that part." I think I'm doing a horrible job at this, but at least I'm honest.

"So, I have to worry about a spurned female dragon in your kingdom?" She sarcastically asks.

I knew I should have mentioned it before. "Currently, she's away visiting her homeland. I plan on having Drake train you in self defence if that is something you are comfortable with." I trust Drake with my life, I know he'd take care of her.

She nods along, listening to what I have to offer.

"When we reach *our* home, we'll discuss the wedding ceremony and mating traditions with her. She'll arrange them for us." I add. Mallory loves decorating and setting things up.

"I'm still getting used to thinking of the Dragon Kingdom as our home. Much less being its queen." She chuckles while shaking her head.

I smile, "Me too." I have never before even thought of having someone to rule beside me. My father had his concubines, my great grandfather ruled with his mate however.

"My mother used to say that the Taegador Kingdom was the most beautiful place she ever saw." Willow whispers, catching my attention.

"Your mother saw the kingdom?" I ask. This is the first I've heard of a human willingly entering the kingdom without either needing somewhere to hide, or to have sex.

"She said she did, not long before she married my father. She used to tell me stories before I went to bed. That was until she got sick and passed." There's a desolate tone in her voice when she speaks about her mom.

I know she misses her. She didn't get to have everything a child should. Every child needs a mothers guidance and love while growing into an adult.

"I'm sorry you lost her at such a young age." I whisper as I reach over and caress her soft cheek. She smiles and leans into my hand.

"Thank you." she whispers back.

I grab her waist with my other hand and pull her towards me. In an instant I have her in my lap. Her back to my chest and her ass pressed firmly into lap.

I nuzzle into her hair, letting her scent wash over me.

If her mom visited the kingdom, it had to be while I was king. Humans rarely lived past 80. Not to mention she died early in life due to an illness.

Unless her mom wasn't human. That couldn't be the case though. Everything about Willow screams human. So *both* her parents had to be human.

I already know King Raguel is human scum, so that's one. "What was your mom like Willow?" I ask. If I want to confirm her moms identity, I have to know what she was like.

"Well, everyone says I look just like her for one. Second, she was adventurous, like me, she always said that she had wanted to see the dragons flying in the sunset or when the moon was full." Content runs through her words when she speaks of her mom.

"I remember her and my father always arguing. I know one time he denied me being his daughter, when he went to strike me, mom jumped in front of me and took the blow." Her voice gives a little of that memory.

So, her father also used to hit her mom. "Why would he deny you being his?" I ask. This could also have something to do with him giving her hand away at eighteen.

"I remember him saying that the dates don't add up. That my mom didn't bleed the night they got married. My father is a cruel man who thinks women are tools for pleasure." she adds, spite in her tone evident when speaking of Raguel.

"She visited the dragons before she got married to your father right?" I ask, this may be useless information to go by, but it's something.

She nods while adding, "My mother spoke of a friend she had made in your kingdom. She always said she missed them, I can't remember their name off the top of my head though."

I nod, rubbing my face farther into her hair. If I knew her friend's name I may be able to find out more. But for now I choose to leave it alone.

"Have I mentioned that you always smell good to me?" I ask, changing the subject.

She giggles, "What do I smell like to you?"

I take a dramatic deep breath and say, "You always smell like hibiscus and smoke from a wildfire to me. Which is a good thing before you start overthinking my Princess."

"How is that a good thing, and how does smoke smell good?" She asks rapidly and turns so she can look me in the face.

I laugh at her sudden outburst. "Well for one, dragons are naturally attracted to smoke. The hibiscus makes it smell sweeter, almost like the flowers can't be touched by the absolute wildfire raging around it."

She is the wildfire though. I believe if she had had the possibility to be an actual princess she'd be a force to be messed with.

I glance toward the window, noting how it's getting dark, we should be approaching Vargas Forest soon. "We will be coming to a stop soon, I don't know about you but I'd love to stretch my legs." Just mentioning stretching my legs makes them cramp.

"That'd be great to me as well. I meant to ask, but does it really get cold at night away from the castle?" Willow asks.

"Depends on the location. Our home stays pretty warm due to the vast amount of dragons. But here, it tends to get a bit nippy for humans." Just that tidbit of information about the outside world has her beaming with curiosity.

Just as I was about to give her more, the carriage came to a stop, the drivers knocking from above us told me we had arrived. "Shall we see the Vargas Forests Village, Princess?" I asked.

She nodded and resumed her sitting position across from me. I opened the door to the carriage and stepped out, using my width to cover the opening of the door.

Taking a breath of the air, I began to smell for any signs of danger. When it was clear there wasn't anything, I stepped away and held my hand out for Willow.

"Princess." I donned as she clapped her small hand in mine and stepped out. Her smile never faltered. I watched as she began to look around at our surroundings.

All around us were trees that looked like they could touch the sky. Their almost red bark was covered in vines that were long just as they were tall.

The birds sang happily in the area, the undergrowth and shrubs were dense beside the pathways. There were houses, shops, inns, taverns, and libraries built into the trees. There was a steady group of people bustling around.

The large trees provided a canopy of shelter for the village when storms came through. Willow was awestruck at the site before us. "It's beautiful." she breathed.

"She is." I murmured while watching her.

"Come, let's retrieve our party and find an inn." I whispered into her ear, turning her attention away from the trees and back to me. She nodded and walked with me, never letting go of my hand.

I approached a carriage that smelled of dragon and a very stressed human and knocked on it. Looking at a carriage behind it, I watched as Winslow stepped out.

The door to the carriage opened and Lila, Willow's maid, made a very rushed exit while Drake was roaring with laughter. Lila began fuming while she came to stand behind a now curious Willow.

Then, Drake exited the carriage. "I'm glad to see you two are getting somewhat along." I sighed as I watched the two of them. I can see a dynamic forming there, the type of it, though, I'm not sure of.

"Well, let's find an inn that will feed and give us a bed for the night." Winslow added, ruining the moment. Giving him a stale look I nodded.

It didn't take long to find an inn, for the right price that is. We all sat at a large table and waited for a waitress to bring us our meals and drinks.

I sat on the left of Willow, Lila on her right, Drake on Lilas right, then Winslow.

"So, Princess Willow, tell me. How did you learn of all the villages?" Winslow began to ask Willow. I noticed she began to rub her palms together under the table, so I grabbed her hands in my right one.

"Well, I read a lot. I've studied maps as well, and have read history books too." She put it all out in a simple form. Winslow nodded, still studying her with his eyes.

"What does your father think of that?" He replied with a question that he knew was touchy. Growling I answered for Willow.

"She doesn't have to answer any of your questions, old man."

Winslow didn't even flinch, but Willow squeezed my hand. "My father is finicky. Reading is actually the only thing I was allowed to do, besides sit in the garden." She replied courtly.

He was getting under her skin. I could feel the anger and panic coming from her.

"Oh look, food is here." Drake said hurriedly as a waitress appeared and began to set various dishes and drinks down.

I grabbed a mug of what smelled like ale and drank it down while shooting daggers at Winslow. All he did was shrug. The dragon sure knew how to push me.

"Tell me Winslow, are you an old man or an old dragon?" Willow asked, taking us all by surprise. Drake choked on his own drink. While I stifled a laugh.

Winslow scoffed and looked away. When I turned to Willow her face was flush red. She stepped outside of her comfort zone and it surprised and embarrassed herself.

"Let's eat and find our rooms." I said with a chuckle. I was proud she achieved that goal for herself.

Willow sipped on her ale after she finished her rabbit stew. Drake kept picking at Lila who took up arms ignoring him, which only worked in his favor. Winslow decided to finally stay quiet, but I knew he was listening.

"Well, I think it's time I retired for the night. Will you be nearby?" Willow asked me in a hushed tone. She didn't want some old dragon eavesdropping.

"I will always be near you Princess. Come let's find our room." I replied. I grabbed her hand and helped her from her seat. The others began to follow suit. I led her through the crowd and to the stairs that led to the rooms.

Hopefully they'd have rooms that were open and close to each other. That way I'd be close if something happened. I made sure to keep Willow close to me while we headed to the stairs.

When we were able to make it to the top, we began to look for the available rooms. Willow was still in awe about being inside of a tree. "How about these, King Everest?" Drake asked with a pointed look at a few rooms.

I nodded. Willow was the first to pick a room. "Lila will you-" she began to say but I raised my hand, cutting her off mid speech.

"It's fine, Lila, you may go ahead and rest and I'll attend to Princess Willow." I spoke and never let my eyes stray from Willow's own. Her face grew pink but she nodded at Lilas questioning look.

I followed Willow into her room. The room had a bed able to fit two people. A small night stand beside it with a candle that was lit.

Across from the bed was a single desk and chair with a window that had its shutters closed.

"Since I will always be nearby, I don't mind to always assist you in any way possible." I tell her, locking her door behind me.

"Well I don't always want to trouble you, Everest." Her tone was light and playful.

"You, my *queen*, can trouble me all day if you wanted and I would not mind. Even if it kept me up all night."

She smiled and turned to me, "Would you like to lie with me?" She asked. It was my turn to smile.

"I'd love to. But first, you are wearing too much to sleep in dear." I approached as I spoke and began to untie her corset from the front. She'd be wearing a chemise gown underneath that she could sleep in.

Laying her corset on the desk in the room, I returned back to a flustered Willow. I only smiled at her shyness and began to untie her dress laces.

I can hear her heartbeat kick up a notch. "Do not worry Willow. Tonight we will rest. I don't want that nosy Winslow to be able to hear you." I chuckle the words out.

Winslow would undoubtedly be trying to listen to us anyway. Not that I wouldn't love to have Willow writhing and moaning my name underneath me.

Once the dress was loose, I helped her out of it and placed it on the back of the chair across from the bed. Willow had her arms tucked across her chest, hiding herself from me.

"Princess, you need not hide yourself from me, ever. You are the most gorgeous woman I have ever laid my eyes on. Nothing could ever turn me away from you." I gently coax as I approach her.

She smiles softly as I wrap my arms around her waist and lift her. A small squeal escapes her mouth just as I envelop my mouth on her hers.

Chapter Six

Willow

Everest's mouth is on mine. I taste the ale on him. Wrapping my hands around his neck, I tangle my fingers into his hair. His hair is soft like down feathers.

He doesn't let me go until my back is pressed into the mattress. "I could kiss you for eternity Willow." He whispers against my lips. When he pulls away I shiver from the crisp air.

"Are you cold?" he asks, his brows furrowed. I nod. He rises from the bed and kicks his boots off, leaving them to the side. He begins to unbutton his shirt.

Revealing all the corded muscle underneath. His whole body looks like it was carved from stone. His abs lead to an impressive V formation on his hips that dipped low into his waistline.

I raised myself into a sitting position and moved the sheets back from the bed and crawled under them. Even the sheets were cold.

I watched as Everest turned and took his shirt off. His back was now to me as he walked to the desk and placed his shirt over my dress. Even the man's back was covered in muscle.

When he returned to me he got under the sheets with me and pulled me to him. Wrapping his arms around my body.

"I can't have my mate and queen getting sick before we even mate." he mumbled into my hair.

I smiled at how much he cares for me. A man has never showered me this much attention for this long. I turned until I was facing him and snuggled my head under his chin.

He was always warm around me and I loved it. His body felt like it was searing into mine, leaving its own print.

I wondered if we would ever have time to ourselves like this when we made it to the Taegador Kingdom. "Everest?" I questioned.

"Yes Willow?"

"Will we have time together when we reach our destination?" I asked. He is a King after all, so I know he will have a busy schedule with meetings to attend and business to do.

"I will always make time for you. And even if I'm busy, you may always summon me, or even join me if you wanted." he replied.

So he didn't mind if I just casually stepped into his zone. I nodded the best I could while tucked under him. My eyelids were beginning to get heavy.

"Thank you." I managed to mumble before sleep enveloped me.

"Willow baby? Come, let's go see the garden. The flowers should be in full bloom." Mom said as she waved me over from playing with my dolls.

"Coming mommy!" I shouted. She only smiled at me. "Hold my hand, I'll tell you a story while we walk." She playfully tussled my hair.

I was practically bouncing with every step. I loved her stories so much. I want to be just like her when I'm older. I want to see the world just as she had.

"Before I had met your father, I used to be a very adventurous person. I had wanted to see the world, discover new things." She started.

"I once went to Taegador Kingdom, the kingdom of the dragons. It was so beautiful there. The castle is a sight itself to behold." She looked up and out of the castle windows as she spoke.

Almost like she was reminiscing about the past.

"I have a friend that lives there. I'm sure they miss me just as much as I miss them. If you ever, and I mean ever find yourself in the dragon kingdom. Seek them out and they will help you SweetPea." We were now in the garden and she was crouched in front of me.

"Mommy are the dragons nice?" I asked.

She chuckled, "Of course baby, they're better than most humans after all. I wish you could have met my friend, but things happened." her tone was full of sadness when mentioning her friend.

"If you ever meet him you'll know him. He's kind of annoying like a badger. His amber eyes look like fresh honey. He's a good person, but he doesn't let people run him over, and he doesn't believe in hurting women or children." she said as she rubbed my cheek.

"I want to go see him with you when I'm older, mommy. Can we please go?" I begged. She just smiled at my antics.

"WILLOW, IT'S TIME TO wake up." A smooth voice spoke while rubbing my arm. I know that voice belonged to Everest. His voice was always smooth. I groaned and slowly peeled my eyes open.

The memories of my mom are still fresh in my mind. I should probably tell them to Everest, maybe my moms friend was still alive.

"Everest, can I ask you something?" I asked while rubbing the sleep from my eyes.

"Of course you can." he said, when i looked at him he was buttoning his shirt together, his boots already on his feet.

"I remember my mom telling me what her friend used to look like. Could he still be alive if he's a dragon?" I asked. I already know dragons have long lives, as long as they know how to defend and protect themselves.

I could tell he was thinking. "Yes, as long as nothing has happened to them, what did they look like?" he replied.

"My mom told me that he had amber eyes, and that he was annoying like a badger." I'm not entirely sure how my mom made that comparison.

Looking at Everest's face, his brows were deeply furrowed and his eyes calculating. "Are you sure that's what you remember?" He asked as he came to stand in front of me.

I nod slowly. What's he getting at? "I'll talk to Drake and Winslow about it. Winslow is one of the oldest dragons so he would remember a dragon with amber eyes. That color is rare, and I only know of one dragon that has them." He spoke as he helped me up from the bed.

He already had my dress and corset laid onto the bed.

"Okay" I mumbled.

He helped me into my dress, fastening it just how it was yesterday and doing the same with the corset. We'll be heading toward Salas Village today.

We'll have to camp outside of their village since they aren't privy to outsiders.

During breakfast, the men were quiet. Most likely using their mind links. I noticed Winslow glancing at me a few times, so I know I was the topic.

Even Drake who was chipper yesterday was now even quiet. None of us even spoke as we paid our tab and headed to the carriages. I didn't want to bother Everest while he was in his private mind meeting.

Sitting in the carriage across from a seriously too quiet Everest, I looked out of the window.

When Everest cleared his throat I jumped, not expecting it. "Sorry. I talked to the others and we all agreed to only knowing of one amber eyed dragon. But, it's not a happy story." he crossed his arms and slouched back.

"What do you mean?" I asked

"Well, his name is Vance. His title, however, is 'The BloodThirsty'. He controlled many generations of the army and guardsmen. He is *the* oldest dragon alive. Before Zephyra had me in her sights, it was Vance." I shivered when he spoke.

"He always turned her down, saying he loved someone else. Then, one day he went mad, he lost control and shifted into his dragon. It took a lot of us to restrain him. We had to lock him in a cell." He sighed and rubbed his face.

"He's still in his dragon form today. He refuses to talk to anyone. His dragon wont let anyone close enough." he shrugged.

So there's that. My moms friend is most likely insane now. I doubt Everest would let me near an out of control dragon, especially a male.

"I wouldn't be able to see him would I?" I asked. Everest looked away and shook his head.

"No. It's too dangerous. He could kill you and not realize what he's done." His gentle tone told me he was more worried about my safety.

"It's okay. I understand." I smiled at him.

Mom had said that he was a caring person. But would he be the way she remembered if he wasn't his dragon now? How else would I meet him since he's a dragon?

"What was he like when he went mad?" I asked quickly. Surprising Everest.

"Well, he was easy going and aggravating as hell. Being the oldest dragon he was once respected. During times of war, his dragon could appear in people's dreams and kill them from the inside out. That's how he got his title." Everest shrugged one shoulder while thinking of Vance.

"He is as strong as me, so there once was a debate about who could rule better. But Vance didn't want to be king. But if the man doesn't show or eat, after a while, he'll get sick." Everest was looking at me now.

"That's what we are all hoping for to be honest. We know it's cruel but it's the only way to force him to shift back into a man." So they want him to shift back just as much as I do.

"Why did he go mad, was it an illness?" I asked Everest. I'm hoping I get the answers I need. I want to know more of my mom in any way that I can.

I lost her when I was a kid. My father tried to hit me when she was around, but she took the blow for me. When she died, that's when he really got bad about hitting.

I don't think my mom ever really loved him anyway, I know I never have.

"We're not really sure why he went mad. All he did was yell that he lost someone he cared for." Everest said as he repositioned his legs.

I nod at him.

We stay quiet for a long time until I yawn. It catches Everest's attention who smiles, "Come here Willow." He beckons while patting his lap.

Blushing I rise from my seat and position my legs between Everest's own, sitting on one of his massive thighs. He nuzzles his way to the crook of my neck, rubbing his lips where my shoulder and neck meet.

Then he surprises me by licking from there up to right below my ear where he bites and sucks on the skin. I lean into him and whimper.

His hands find their way to my waist and squeeze. "You taste amazing Willow." he whispers to me.

"Everest." I murmur.

"What is it?" he questions.

"They'll hear us." I say while placing my hands on his shoulders.

"I've already told them to shut down that nosy business of theirs, I want you to cum for me." he chuckles at me, his voice hoarse.

I can feel how hard he is against my thigh. He's really big right there.

He shucks up my dress so he can get a hand under my skirts. His touch against my thighs has me rubbing them together.

"I can smell you Willow. You smell divine." he praises.

In one swift motion, he grabs my right thigh, lifts me, and has me straddling his lap. He raises his hand and squeezes my right ass cheek.

His mouth still works on my neck. Licking and biting in places that make me squirm. He pulls my waist down until his firm bulge is up against my center. I inhale a breath at the friction.

"When I take you, I'm going to want you every hour. I already want you every hour." he whispers again.

"Everest," I moan.

He moves my hips up and down. Causing me to rub myself against him. My breathing is beginning to become frantic and uneven.

This feels amazing. Is this what it will be like when we have sex the first time?

He moves his head to look at my face which I'm sure is flustered.

But this time, instead of him kissing me first.

I kissed him.

It was a fast move that he quickly controlled. His tongue darted out and teased my lips. I opened my mouth and allowed entry to his tongue that battled mine for dominance.

I moaned into his mouth.

Now both of his hands were on my ass, squeezing and using them to move my hips over his erect appendage.

"Fuck Willow." he groans.

I want him to make that sound again. I tangle my fingers in his hair and pull gently. He growls and continues his assault on my mouth.

"Everest, I want more, please." I beg him.

I want to feel this man underneath me. I want him to always want me. I *want* him to make more sounds.

"Yes Princess." he growls

One of his hands moves until his fingers land on my clit. His finger pad rubs over it causing me to moan. He's still moving me up and down his covered shaft, but playing with my clit at the same time.

His mouth covers mine again, and this time I battle his own tongue for dominance. I suck his lip into my mouth and nip at him, causing him to groan again.

"Princess, this is a dangerous game," he says. But I don't care how dangerous it is, I want him and I want him now.

"I want you, Everest." I whisper against his mouth continuing my own assault while he plays with my clit. Causing friction from both his finger and his appendage.

"Shit." he curses under his breath.

"I'm not taking your virginity in this damn carriage, but I'll give you something." His hands move away from my body but his lips don't leave mine.

In that moment I hear his belt clicking loose, followed by the popping sound of buttons. Something large lands against my stomach. I know what it is even though I can't see it.

Everest pulls away and repositions himself under me. He pulls me closer to him, and sets me back down.

His cock is now under my pussy. I inhale slowly and find his eyes. "I'm not taking you in here, but I'll give you a taste." he says as grabs the back of my neck and pulls my mouth back to his.

Using his other hand he moves me slowly down him. The new feeling caused waves of pleasure through me.

"That's it." he whispers.

Pulling away once more, he bites, kisses, and licks my throat and collar bone.

"Oh Everest." I moan, angling my head to give him better access.

Just feeling him without any barriers between us is amazing. Every little motion has me getting closer to the edge.

"Fuck Willow. You feel amazing, even if I'm not inside you." Everest praises, sending me closer.

"Everest, I want more." I continue to beg.

Everest picks up the pace by rubbing me faster on him. Whimpering, I wrap my arms tighter around him.

"That's it baby, cum for me." he pleads.

"Everest, I'm close." I whine. He groans as he continues to increase the pace.

He bites down on my shoulder through the sleeve of my dress, causing the last push I need.

Moaning, my legs begin to tingling and everything feels like it's locked up tight as the euphoric blast of pleasure rolls through me.

Everest growls as he stills. He pulls me close to him, tucking my head under his chest and wrapping his arms around me, letting me ride out the waves.

I'm a panting mess and so is Everest.

"I didn't hurt you did I?" He asks, sincerity in his voice.

"No, it was amazing. I like when you make those sounds." I whisper the last part and feel like I could shrink in on myself.

Everest laughs, the rumbling sound from his chest vibrating me, "Don't worry Princess, I like when you make those sounds too."

I thought those sounds didn't sound like me, myself. I've realized that I'd make those sounds all day for him as long as he makes them for me.

"We'll find somewhere to bathe when we come to a stop. I'm sorry I didn't think of the mess we'd make." He apologizes. He's the only man in my life, besides the guards that used to follow me, that actually apologizes.

"I love how you always accept your actions and apologize like a man with decency." I said to him, tilting my head just enough to see his face.

He looks down at me, "Any man should when in the presence of a lady." he says before kissing my forehead.

"I know you're tired after all of that, so how about you nap since you're comfortable and I'll wake you when we stop?" he offered.

I liked the sound of that. "Okay."

Chapter Seven

Everest

Willow had finally fallen asleep in my arms. She was snoring softly when I felt the subconscious knock in my mind. Opening up, I knew it was Drake.

"We will be approaching the outside of Salas soon," he mentioned.

"Good, if it is still there, I plan to show WIllow the hotspring." I informed him. Drake, no doubt, would smell the sex on us and tease us for it.

"Aw, did someone get a little nitty and gritty?" he teased.

Growling I quickly shut him out of my mind. He would do it anyway so it doesn't matter. He's probably laughing his balls off.

Drake is always the one to tease and pick at people for fun. But when it comes down to it, he can be ruthless and cold.

I still haven't wrapped my head around how Vance plays a part in Willow's life, or her moms for that matter. I'll have to find out more at a later time.

Currently I have other issues. One consisted of wanting to wake Willow and have a repeat of what just happened. The other, figuring out how to evade Zephyra once we were home.

If possible, I could talk to Mallory and see if we can have the ceremonies moved to a closer date.

Just in case Willow doesn't completely agree to train with Drake, having our ceremony closer will provide her with strength when Zephyra decides to act out.

Not only that, but I will also be able to feel Willow if anything were to happen. Her pain would become my own pain.

If anything were to fatally happen to her before our ceremony, I'd kill anyone who stood in my way.

Then, I'd die just to be with her in the afterlife.

If what Willow said, about her father and mother arguing about her mother not bleeding when she wed Raguel, were true, then who was Willow's father really?

If Vance was friends with her mom, he'll have the answers I need. I'm hoping that since he hasn't eaten in decades he'll get sick soon.

Then I will be able to force him to shift back into a man. Willow may not be human, even though everything about her seems human.

There are so many possibilities floating around which makes it hard to come to a conclusion.

I don't want Willow to even be near Vance in his current state. There is a high possibility that he is no longer a man underneath.

If he does show signs of still being a man, then maybe, a very slim fucking maybe.

Sighing, I began to smooth out Willow's hair. Even though her hair is a curly mess now, she's still beautiful.

"Princess," I sooth.

She furrows her brows and attempts to snuggle her way deeper in my chest.

"Willow, it's time to get up Princess." I sooth again trying to gently wake her.

I watch as she inhales a deep breath and slowly cracks one eyelid open. Smiling at her a brush a few stray strands of her curls off her face.

"We're about to be outside of Salas. I have somewhere I want to show you." I whisper as I rub her cheek. She nods, and raises herself up. Thankfully I've already tucked my cock into my pants.

"Good morning gorgeous queen of mine." I tease with a smile.

She smiles and rubs her eyes. "Thank you for waking me." She whispers. I watch as she attempts to straighten her dress.

"Has anyone ever told you that you are beautiful when you first wake up?" I ask her.

She looks at me with wide stunned eyes. Glancing around she shakes her head and I watch her cheeks turn color.

"Drake, have lila gather a dress for Willow, and you grab me a change of clothes will you. I'm taking Willow for a soak." I order in my head.

When the carriage comes to a stop Willow and I idle in small talk until a small knock comes from the door.

"Your clothes, my lady and lord." A shy voice echoes through.

Willow looks at me with raised brows and I shrug a shoulder with a smile.

"Thank you Lila. We'll be out shortly." I say back to her. I listen and wait for her footsteps to recede. Opening the carriage door I step out and pick the folded clothes up.

"Willow," I beckon just as her head peeks through the carriage door.

"Oh wow, it's beautiful out here." she whispers, stepping out from the carriage.

I nod. All around us is nothing but pure forest untouched by civilization. The birds chirp and sing their songs, the butterflies flutter around searching for flowers. The trees and shrubs are vibrant green, full of life.

I hold my elbow out for Willow to loop her arm around. Then we start walking away from the carriages and their drivers.

"Where I'm taking you, is a natural hot spring. That way we can wash." I tell her in a gentle, all knowing tone.

"Oh really." she giggles. I give her a showy curt nod.

"Of course Princess." I tease.

The ground here is soft and has rich soil. As long as people leave it alone, it'll stay beautiful and rich. Full of life.

Willow and I continue to walk until I start smelling the water. "Close your eyes for me?" I ask her. She gives me a puzzled look but closes her eyes. Grabbing her hands I start to guide her to the hotspring.

The hotspring sits atop a cliff that overlooks the Northern Kingdom. You can even see her fathers castle from here. Steam rises from the pool of water.

Setting the clothes where they wont get wet, I walk behind Willow and hold her waist.

"You can open them now." I whisper against her ear. She shivers. I hear her breath hitch at the sight before us.

"How about we bathe and admire its beauty, while I admire someone else's beauty." I whisper against the nape of her neck.

She nods her head and steps forward to the water. I begin to untie the back of her corset and dress.

She holds the front of her dress against herself. Her dress, open in the back revealing her scars. The scars, no doubt, came from a whip.

I rub the palm of my hand down her back and watch the goosebumps rise. "You will always be the most beautiful woman I've ever laid eyes on." I whisper.

"Thank you Everest." She replies.

Stepping away from her, I unbutton my shirt, tossing it to the side. "Are you going to join me?" I tease.

She smiles but her blushing doesn't cease. I unbutton my pants and they shimmy down my legs to my feet. I catch a glimpse of Willow's face before I turn and enter the hot water.

Her eyes wide and mouth slightly agape, she watches me from the rocks. I make my way across the small pool and lower myself into the water until I feel it at the bottom of my chin.

"Well?" I beckon her.

She swallows a lump in her throat and lets her dress fall to the ground. I see her rosy nipples through her chemise gown. She slowly lets it fall to the ground after her dress.

In front of me, completely naked and utterly goddess-like, is the woman who holds the key to my beating heart.

I watch as she wraps her arms around her waist and tests the water with a toe. When she's sure of herself she eventually steps in.

She's arms reach away but I give her space until she no longer feels the need to hide herself from me.

"Is it to your liking or shall I make it warmer for you?" I question her. I always could use the dragon inside me to emit more heat and heat the water up to however she liked it.

The heat didn't bother us dragon shifters, neither did the cold. We always could live in any condition besides having fatal wounds.

"No, this is perfect actually. Thank you though." She mumbles.

She looks around us, taking everything in, as I slowly make my way towards her. My cock already pulsing between my legs.

Wrapping my arms around her waist I pull her back towards me. I know she fills my hardness against her backside from the way that she jumps.

I let her relax in my arms until she laid her head back against my shoulder.

"Everest?" She calls my name. I hum in response and watch her.

Her pulse beats violently from her throat and I feel her fiddling with her thumbs.

I drag my hands from her waist up to her supple breasts and give them a gentle squeeze, letting my fingers run across her nipples.

I lower my head in the crook of her shoulder and bite her flesh, not hard enough to leave my mating mark.

She arches her back in response and sucks her lip between her teeth.

"I've told you that these are mine to bite and suck on." I tell her while using my thumb to pull her lip out. Her tongue darts out and licks the tip of my finger.

Growling in response I hold her tighter, my cock throbbing painfully against her ass.

I drag my other hand lower and tease her clit. She bucks and moans in my grasp. "Tell me what you want, Princess." I tease.

"Do you want me here?" I ask while barely flicking her clit.

Her mouth opens and she nods her head.

"Good. Do you want me to make you come?" I ask. I lick the outer shell of her ear and she squirms.

"Tell me Princess." I coax.

"Yes Everest, please." she pleads.

I dip my fingers into her needy little cunt. Her breath catches and the flush creeps down her chest. I continue to dip them in and out, listening to her breathy moans.

Her hand reaches around to the back of my head, gripping my hair and giving it a slight tug.

Growling in her ear I say, "Careful Princess, this dragon doesn't do well with reins."

Her lip trembles and I know she's close. I scoop her up and turn her to face me. Stradling me, she braces herself with her hands on my chest.

I crave every touch from the woman in front of me, I crave every sound she'll make for me, I crave everything from her.

Claiming her mouth with mine, she sinks into me. I grip the back of her neck and hold her close. Feeling her nipples rub across my chest, I growl. The vibration, I know, travels straight through her.

"Everest, I want to come." She pleads against me.

"Yes my queen." I replied.

Reaching between us, I fist my cock and tease her entrance with the head.

"It's going to sting and feel like a pinch at first, but it'll get better." I promise her.

She nods, and I slowly push myself into her. Her walls spasm against my cock, until I feel that small barrier inside her.

Willow scrapes her nails down my back and mewls.

I give another push until I fully sink into her.

"That's it Princess. You did so well." I praise.

I give her a moment to adjust to me being seated so far inside of her. My cock throbs with the need of release.

When her muscles relax, I grip her ass cheeks and give a firm but gentle squeeze.

I slowly raise her and seat her back down on myself. Making sure not to hurt her for her first time.

After a few more motions, she begins to move herself the way I'm doing it. When I'm sure she catches on, I remove one hand and caress her cheek, rubbing below her eye.

"Fuck Princess. You feel even better when I'm inside of you." I praise again.

"Everest, you feel so deep." She moans.

I feel deep because I am. Dragons are a lot bigger than humans. A lot of human whores find their way into my kingdom to chase a dragon around, all saying that having sex with a dragon is better than an average man.

I bite and suck on her flesh above her breasts, over her heart. Marking my territory. If I could stay like this with her, I'd be a happy man.

The way she spasms around me sends me closer over the edge. I use my other hand to rub small circles over her clit.

Willow arches her back with a long breathy moan escaping her lips.

"Yes Princess, that's it. Take all of me." I whisper to her. The sound of moaning mingled with skin slapping skin, sloshing in the water echoes around us.

"Everest I'm so close." Willow whines.

Her eyes are hazy and her pupils are blown.

"Me too Princess." I grunt. I lean my head back, grinding my teeth. I could lose myself at any moment inside of her, but she needs to come first.

Her hands grip my shoulders. I watch her pulse thump in her neck. I feel her walls spasm and clench around my cock. Her muscles stiffen and her breath hitches with every moan escaping her.

"Let go Princess." I whisper and claim her lips with mine, drowning out her moans as she orgasms.

Growling I feel my own release bubbling. I wrap my arms around her and hold her close as my own orgasms rips through me.

Chapter Eight

Willow

ALL I COULD THINK ABOUT was the man, or dragon, who took my virginity in a hot spring. The one who apologizes to me, who worships the ground I walk on. The one who will kneel before me and pledge his every breath to me.

Last night was the best night. Everest and I slept under the stars after having sex many times. I never got cold with him around, so we slept on a bed of moss and used our dirty clothes as pillows.

Currently , we are approaching the Taegador Kingdom. Home of the dragons. Everest's kingdom and home, and eventually mine too. A place where we would, maybe one day, raise our children together.

"Look up at the sky." Everest whispers from beside me.

Moving the curtain from the carriage window I look around the sky. What looks like little dots are moving towards us.

But they're not dots, as they get closer I see the large wingspans and elongated necks with toothy muzzles.

"Dragons." I say in a hushed tone.

The two dragons swoop low enough the wind moves the wagon. There's a red dragon and a stony grey one.

The stony grey dragon has a scar that travels down their neck. The red one is a fiery color that looks almost feminine.

"They are gorgeous." I squeal at Everest as he laughs.

"The red one is Mallory, my sister. The grey one is Darcian, he's her escort." He points to each one individually.

Above us, the two dragons roar and grumble at one another.

"They look so happy flying." I look at the dragons in wonder.

"Of course they do, a dragon is built to claim the skies after all." he says and looks at the two above us with longing.

"Do you want to join them? I'll be alright." I shrug and motion above us. He smiles at me but shakes his head.

Before I can say anything, Everest's face turns into a stony contrast. The exact opposite of how he just was. A low guttural growl escapes him.

Placing my hand over his I wait for him to speak.

"Princess, when the carriage comes to a stop, do not leave it. Don't look outside no matter what you hear. Don't do anything until I say it is safe, okay?" he grasps my hands, his eyes warring with emotion and anger.

"What's going on Everest?" I plead but he just shakes his head.

When the carriage comes to a stop, I hear what sounds like thousands of dragons roaring and growling.

Giving me a kiss on my forehead, Everest turns and leaves the carriage.

"Do not leave this carriage. I will come for you." Everest voice echoes around me. It's his voice while he's a dragon.

A powerful dominant roar vibrates me from outside the carriage before what feels like a large gust of wind shakes it.

Trembling, I hold myself.

"It's going to be okay." I tell myself over and over. Whatever is going on outside has to be bad enough Everest needed to shift and told me to stay put.

A screeching roar makes me cover my ears and whimper.

"So some human princess decided she was good enough to be the queen of a thousand dragons." a female voice echoes around me.

I don't know any female dragons besides the red dragon I just saw.

"Enough, Zephyra. You have just started a war inside the Taegador Kingdom and a war with King Everest, Lord of the dragons." a male voice chimes in.

I may not know the other voice but I do know the male is Drake's voice. Everest must have sent him.

"You must know, to strike down the future queen of dragons and Everest's chosen mate is punishable by death." Drake informs her in a stoic voice.

"Boy, you don't think I know the rules. If I can't have him then she can't either. She's mortal, a future wound on this kingdom if Everest makes her queen and mate!" her voice screeches just as I'm flying across the carriage.

Swallowing my scream as I feel my head hit something. Everything I see is blurred and almost moving.

Groaning, I crowd in on myself. Everything hurts.

"Willow!" Drake roars.

I managed to look around the carriage. The windows are shattered, and the carriage is upside down.

I know Everest, said not to go anywhere but now I don't have a choice but to run. To run away from the spurned dragon who wanted the title of Queen and Mate to the Lord of the Dragons.

Crawling towards the window, I make a silent prayer that Zephyra doesn't see me. It takes all the courage I have to lift myself to my feet and run like I have never before.

If I wasn't in this situation, I would take the time to admire the scenery and beauty of the place. But now, my feet attempt to carry me far away from the dragon who is out for my life.

From the looks of it, I'm in the citadel. Everywhere I turn there are numerous dragons fighting one another. Some lay on the ground dying or injured.

Ahead, there's a cave that doesn't have anyone blocking the entrance. I don't know why I do it, but I run straight for the cave.

Maybe it's the adrenaline or maybe it's because I'm scared without Everest.

With a scream I dodge talons and tails. Entering the cave it takes a moment for my eyes to adjust to the darkness. But the dark doesn't stop me from running for my literal life. I turn several corners until I can't run anymore.

My lungs feel ice cold and like they are about to shrink in on themselves. My breathing is erratic and my heart thunders like that of thousands of galloping horses.

I cough and wheeze for breath.

Not knowing where I am, I lean on the wall for support. My feet hurt and my toes feel like they're about to fall off.

I walk alongside the wall feeling for any corners to turn down. I can still hear the many dragons fighting, echoing throughout the cave system.

Unable to bear it anymore, I collapsed against the stone wall.

A waft of warm air feels like it wraps itself around me. Closing my eyes, the air feels like home. A sense of familiarity wrapped in itself.

Sighing and leaning my head back, I let the tears fall. Unable to make too much noise and risk being caught by Zephyra and whoever else is on her side.

I've never even met the lady and she's hunting me down the very moment I arrive in Taegador. I hug my knees to my chest and cry in silence.

"Why do you cry, Klaudia?" a warm smooth male voice like honey wrapped around me, startling me.

Rising to my feet, I look around for the voice. Holding my hands to my chest.

They just said my mothers name.

"W-who are you and how do you know my mom?" I demand. Even though I'm not one to demand answers.

I don't even look the part to demand for answers.

"Are you not her? You have to be her, you look just like her." The voice replies.

I turn and walk towards the voice.

"No, my mother died when I was a small child. She had a foreign illness that she succumbed to. Now, who are you!?" I raise my faltering voice. I'm scared but refuse to show it.

"Klaudia could not have died. She was not mortal. No mortal illness could have just killed an elder dragon."

What did he just say?

"Who are you and how do you know my mother!" I scream at the voice, storming over to it.

I come to a stop when I see large cell-like doors and chains holding a large golden dragon to the ground. His head is adorned in many small spikes that cradle two impala-like horns.

His amber gold eyes watch me with sadness.

"Vance." One word and one name leave my mouth.

"Are you a witch? Who decided to dress up as the love of my life and torment me?" His voice was raspy, if he had the ability left to growl I'm sure he would.

"N-no. My name is Willow. I'm Klaudia's only child and daughter. She married King Raguel and had me. But she died when I was six." The tears haven't stopped flowing yet.

The warmth of them trailing down my face.

"You're wrong you know? Klaudia and I were going to be mates, she was barely pregnant when she left me. Some pompous King threatened her family in the south if she didn't marry him." His eyes studied me as he spoke.

This doesn't make any sense. "I don't understand what you are saying." I flail my arms about. Making an exasperated show.

"I'm too weak to enter your dreams or I'd show you. You smell like a familiar dragon, and you're bleeding. I can hear fighting outside. What happened, child?" he questions with a snorting sigh.

Mother said I could trust Vance but Everest said not to in his current state.

Rubbing my pounding forehead I make a decision, even if it's unwise.

"King Raguel, the man who is supposed to be my father, sold me the night of my eighteenth birthday. King Everest, your king, bought me. I'm to be his queen and mate." I watch the dragon's eyes glimmer, catching whatever light is in the cave.

"When we arrived here, dragons all around us started fighting. Zephyra is hunting me down. She wants me dead. She's wanted Everest and the title of queen since I don't know when." I shrug my shoulders.

"It's the power that comes from being his mate and queen she wants. Why would your father sell you?" Vance adds.

I decide to sit in front of the dragon with the cell bars in between us.

"My father believes I'm not his daughter. He always said something about the time that didn't add up and that mother didn't bleed the night they wed." Looking back at it now, I don't even think the time leading to my birth added up either.

The dragon makes a slight move with his head, the chains rattling. His eyes watch beyond me.

"Hide, Willow." His raspy voice whispers.

Standing up, I look around frantically. There's nowhere in this cave to hide, except-

I slide myself between the bars holding Vance in his cell and gently tuck myself under his wing.

Now that I'm close to him, I see just what kind of state he is in.

His ribs are bare and showing through his scales. Where the chains are wrapped around his neck, legs, and tail, are raw marks from years of fighting to break them.

His pretty golden scales are diluted in color in some places, giving him a patchy look. His body is marred with many scars in different places, probably from his time fighting in wars.

Hugging my knees to my chest under his wing, Vance moves slightly to readjust his wing. Tucking me closer to him.

The heat that a dragon would usually emit is faint from him.

"Oh Princess, where are you?" Zephyra's voice echoes through the cave in a sing-song voice.

I can hear her talons scraping the stone ground until it's right outside Vance's cell.

"Poor dragon. Locked away to rot and deteriorate. No longer The BloodThirsty are you? Have you seen the princess? I can smell her putride blood." Zephyra growls, her tail whipping in the air behind her.

I don't know where Everest is. Surely he'd be looking for me by now?

"You should leave Zephyra. Your crime today is punishable by death." Vance's voice carries forth. He sounds like he's trying to be a strong and dominant dragon. In his current state he may be far from that.

"Oh, so you can still speak, hm. You've just been playing dumb this whole time." Zephyra chuckles. The sound is menacing from where I'm safely tucked away at.

I place my hand on Vance's side providing comfort.

"I've lost the love of my life, the one who I was going to mate. And you are hunting her daughter. You think I will give you Klaudia's only child?" Vance actually growls this time. The sound vibrates the loose pebbles on the ground.

Chapter Nine

Everest

I'VE LEFT WILLOW IN Drake's care. When Mallory sent me a mind link, Zephyra had started fighting my guards. She brought dragons from her clan to fight alongside her.

How she heard of Willow and I pairing, I'm not sure. But I will find out.

Pulling my talons from some male dragon's chest, I watch life fade from his eyes. Zephyra and her clan will pay for coming on my land and causing bloodshed.

Most of her clan was either dead or dying out.

"Everest! Drake's been severely wounded and Zephyra's went into the cave!" Mallory drills into my head.

Only one thought consumed my head.

Willow.

"Mal I need you to get to her right now. I have to find Princess Willow!" I growl. With an anger consuming roar I lift myself into the skies. My wings beating heavily.

I reach the citadel and spot Drake unmoving. The carriage that Willow and I arrived in together now turned upside down, the glass windows shattered and part of it charred to a crisp.

"Drake, are you alright, where is Willow?" I command. Drake's black dragon has an open wound on his belly, his wings are torn to shreds, beside him Lila wipes her tear stained cheeks.

"She ran into the cave after Zephyra flipped the carriage. I tried to stop her but Zephyra went in after her. Everest,Vance is in there." Drake's green eyes land on the mouth of the cave.

No. With Vance unstable and Zephyra out for blood, Willow can't survive the both of them without being mated to me.

Without another word to Drake or from Drake, I run towards the mouth of the cave, catching Willow's scent and Zephyra's on top.

Surely Willow wouldn't have gone into Vance's cell. My talons scrape the stone floor of the cave.

When the two scents get stronger I crouch and crawl alongside the stone, staying close to the wall.

The predatory hunting instincts kicking in, my breathing slows. Spreading my talons along the ground to minimize sound.

Turning my head around a corner before the rest of my body, I spot Vance laying in his cell.

In front of him, Mallory and Zephyra circle one another.

Willow is nowhere in sight but her scent doesn't leave the area. My eyes catch movement from Vance's left wing. My sight zeroes in on a small pale hand and ocean blue eyes peeking from below his wing.

Willow.

She's hiding underneath Vance and he isn't trying to kill her. He isn't moving at all, just watching the two female dragons in front of him, like I'm doing now.

Bolting from my position, I head straight for Zephyra. Leaping over Mallory with hot dragon fire out of my mouth.

She uses her wings to block the fire.

"Well, if it isn't the young lord. Afraid I'll kill the only two women in our life?" she antagonizes.

"Enough of this Zephyra. I have played your game for too long and I'm beginning to grow sick of it and you." I growl. My tail swings to either side of me.

"Aw, I was hoping you'd begin to see my side of the story. I've loved you all these years and you go and choose a pathetic human!" She bellows with a roar, stomping her talons into the stone.

"That woman is not pathetic. She's stronger than you ever could be. Unlike you she wears her scars on the outside but doesn't let it cloud her judgement. You never loved me, you loved the power that would come with me." I tell her, attempting to keep her occupied so I can get closer.

"She's a human Everest! She's frail, she can get sick and die, and then you would die. And then all of Taegador would be without a queen!" She whines. The sound is ear piercing coming from a dragon.

"She's not a human, you idiots." Vance states.

His voice caught us by surprise. We all turn our heads in unison and I use the moment to my advantage.

Lunging forward I wrap my muzzle around her neck. Causing both of us to fall forward.

"Get the hell off of me!" Zephyra cries and struggles beneath my large frame.

Placing my talons on her chest, I squeeze my jaw tighter. The metallic tang of blood filling my mouth.

All the while I sink my talons into her chest, piercing her heart.

Blood spurts from her mouth, causing her to choke. The gurgling sound is sickly.

Zephyra stills underneath me, and I clap my maw tighter, crushing all the bones in her neck.

"Everest?" A small meek voice comes from behind me.

Snapping my blood covered head around, I spot Willow.

Vance has his wing raised, revealing Willow who was safely tucked beside him.

"Princess, I thought," I couldn't finish the words as she ran straight for me. Slipping between the bars and hugging my head to her chest.

"I did too." She whispers. Her tear stained cheeks are dirty, her eyes red rimmed, and the tears falling from her eyes are warm and salty.

"You'll be covered in blood, Willow." I gently warn her, trying to pull myself away from her in my dragon form.

Laughing she says, "I'm already covered in some, even if it's my own."

I look beyond her and spot a worn out looking Vance now standing, his eyes watching mine and Willow's every movement.

Willow looks between me and Vance and backs away from me.

"Will you shift back, Vance? Or do we have to force you?" I question him.

"I will shift back, now that a part of Klaudia is with me." He grumbles. He raises to his talons, stretching his wings to their full extent.

Vance is the oldest dragon alive and one of the biggest, along with me he is also one of the strongest ones alive. Although, in his current state a roach could topple him.

"I have questions when we get you back to the castle. For now, Mallory will release your chains and let you out." I informed him.

Mallory will bring him to the castle once he shifts back. But for now, I have to get Willow to my chambers and *inspect* her perfect body for wounds.

"Come Willow." I called her.

She places a hand on my neck and walks with a limp beside me. Her feet must be sore or hurt.

I slow my walking, *"Would you like a ride?"* I ask her.

Furrowing her brows, she gives me a questioning look.

Laying my wing out, I lay on the ground. My belly rubbing the dirt and stone.

Her eyebrows raise and she makes an o shape with her mouth.

Slowly she walks over to me, looking unsure of what to do.

"Just climb me Willow. You wont hurt me." I chuckle and she shakes her head at me. She grips the spike on my neck and pulls herself up.

Seating herself where my neck meets my shoulders. When she's comfortable I begin walking again.

"Vance told me he loved my mom before she married my father." She states while rubbing my scales.

"I figured your mother and Vance might have had a romantic relationship before she married King Raguel." I sigh. I wait to see if Willow is angry with me before continuing.

"I wanted to wait until I knew for sure about everything. But from what you have told me, and from how he acted all those years ago, I suspect King Raguel Isn't actually your father." I said to her.

There's the huge possibility that Willow's father is Vanceand that she's half dragon. But even then, she should possess dragon traits, which she doesn't.

Stepping out from the cave, I see Drake now in a crouched position. The other dragons, including Winslow, wait in the citadel for me. A few of them are still in their dragon forms while others have decided to shift back.

Raising to full height and extending my wings out to look bigger I look at all of them.

"I wanted today to be special for all of us. But things don't turn out the way we want them. Zephyra and her clansmen have been defeated today. You all did good in defending your home, I am proud of each of you." My voice carries all around and echoes in the quiet.

Many pairs of eyes find their way to the woman on my back.

"As many of you are wondering, the woman I have with me is Princess Willow. She is going to be my mate and your queen. Her father, a long awaited friend that we have all been waiting on, will be joining us tomorrow night." Some of them look at each other, while the rest whisper.

If willow is a dragon we will have to find out. Maybe, being around other dragons will coax her own dragon out.

Before any outlandish comments or decisions can sprout I decide to make an understanding.

"For anyone else who might decide to cause harm to my family. My mate, or anyone in my kingdom, you should know this, you will end up just like Zephyra did. Dead between my jaws. Or worse, Vance the BloodThirsty will kill you in your sleep." I growl at all of them.

Rendering them silent, I look back at a quiet Willow who's taking it all in.

The brave, shy, beautiful woman who could even command me to my death if she wanted.

Chapter Ten

Willow

Everest had made a public statement to the dragons who waited for us outside the cave.

Laying in the giant bed under a stone ceiling with a large mural of dragons I smile.

I smile because I'm happy, I'm alive, Everest is alive, and Vance may be my father.

Everest voiced his concerns to me about how King Raguel might not be my father. How I may be part dragon but I don't show any outward signs of being one.

Glancing over at a sleeping Everest, I decide to get up and get dressed.

Mallory had told us that she put Vance in a room with plenty of food. She's the fiercest woman I've ever met before. Everest and her spoke of our mating arrangements and ceremonies.

Which was today.

Everest said that it's customary for the two pairs to be separated all day long. I'd be with Mallory shopping for clothes and other things until the time came.

Everest and I chose to wait until a full moon. He noticed how I love watching the full moon on the balcony of our chambers.

Dressing in a baby blue gown and matching corset I open our chamber door.

Spooking myself when a man I've never met before is standing at our door. He's tall and bulky like Everest. His ash hair and medium length beard are a curly mess. But his eyes.

I know those eyes.

"Vance." I smile at him.

"Princess, it's nice to formally meet you. I apologize for spooking you, it was not my attention. However, it is my intention to wake the sleeping beauty over there." He smiles and points over to my bed.

Following his finger, I look at my bed. Where Everest was sleeping, now sits a very grouchy looking and awake Everest.

"Vance. When I released you from your cell, that did not mean to come scaring your queen and king. Or even waking them for that matter." Everest sighs and rubs his face.

I side step and let Vance enter our chambers. Making my way to the desk I sit in the chair that faces the bed.

"Quite the opposite my lord. You knew what would happen. I've been this way since you were a boy. Besides, you have questions and I have answers." Vance shrugs and approaches Everest like he isn't a predator.

Everest growls at the approaching Vance who only chuckles menacingly.

"I have to meet Mallory anyway. I'll see you tonight, Everest." I wave at him and make a hurried escape before I get caught in the crosshairs of two very powerful dragons.

The castle really does have an open concept. The ceiling is high enough to accommodate many dragons in full shift. Most of the rooms have large balconies for dragons to land on.

Adorned on the walls are many silver and blue tapestries, the ceilings are either painted with murals or painted to look like the skies.

Mallory wanted me to meet her in the library. Turning a corner not far from mine and Everest's chambers, I nod at a few guardsmen who are patrolling. They resume a position against the wall with their heads hung low.

Mallory doesn't even look like Everest. But the way they act is the same. Her auburn red hair matches fire, and her emerald colored eyes are like jewels adorned on a crown.

The library has large walls filled to the brim with bookcases and books of many different categories. Everest must have told her how I like to read because she gave me a few of her personal favorites which now sit on the desk in our chambers.

Entering the library I see Drake who is smiling like a toddler and Mallory who is seething.

"Good morning." I chime as I close the door.

Drake bows his head and Mallory clasps her hands with a smile.

"Good morning Princess. Drake, who has taken it upon himself, has decided to be our escort today since Darcian is still healing." She throws Drake a side glance which speaks volumes.

He must antagonize her just as much as he did Lila the night in Vargas Forest.

"Well, that will be quite alright as long as he's okay with hearing women talk about women things." I give him a pointed look.

Smiling he points at Mallory and I, "I know exactly how you talk. Like thieves who stole candy from a child when you are alone with each other."

Laughing and shaking her head Mallory walks over to me and hooks her arm in mine.

We giggle like a pair of children while talking about Everest. She doesn't mention about the day Zephyra attacked us all.

Drake remains unfazed behind us as we walk through the castle and into the citadel. Many of the shops here have opened up and resumed their usual business.

The citadel is grassy but has stone in some places. The shops are built similar to the ones in the Northern Kingdom.

Wildflowers grow sporadically in random spots here and there. They even grow in between the stone cracks in the walkways.

"So what color dress have you decided on?" Mallory asks, taking my attention away from the citadel.

"Well, I think I'd like to go with a gold-colored day-like gown. But, I want to keep an open mind in case there's something else I like." I tell her while brushing my hair out of my face.

She nods and leads me into a dress maker's shop.

"Hello Mrs. Willoughby. This is Princess Willow, Everest's mate." Mallory waves at a woman who sits behind the counter sewing fabric together.

I give a small smile and wave at her. She rises from her position and smooths out her dress.

"If I knew I would have had my Queen to be in here today, I would have cleaned the place up." She laughs and walks over to me.

Giving me a formal bow.

"Please, help yourselves and let me know if there's anything I can help you ladies with." She waves around at all the dresses and gowns.

Mallory takes me to where some beautifully colored gowns are and points out a few. There are dresses of many different colors and varieties.

A crimson gown catches my eye out of the rest of them. Upon closer inspection, the gown looks similar to the blue one Everest had told me to pack but was lost the day I got here.

The difference was that instead of having an almost open chest, it had two slits on the sides from the top of the thigh down.

It had loose fabric around the chest area and ruffled sleeves that hung low on the shoulders.

I grab the hanger it's on and rub the fabric between my fingers. It's soft, like buttery silk.

"Now that's an amazing choice you have there." Mrs. Willoughby sighs as she approaches us.

"How about this one Mallory?" I ask and hold the dress in front of me.

She nods and looks like she's thinking for a moment.

"That will do perfectly. We have some jewels and shoes back at the castle. Do you have some gloves that match?" Mallory asks the woman.

The woman smiles and hurries around the store while we wait. The woman returns with a matching pair of gloves that reach right above my elbow.

"We'll take these please ma'am." Mallory beams.

Mrs. Willoughby wraps the dress and gloves in paper and then puts them into a box wrapped in a silver bow.

We say our goodbyes and head back to the castle where Mallory says she has a few jewels put away.

"So how is Darcian?" I ask her as we walk up the steps to the castle.

"He's going to be alright. The fool got himself into this when he blocked another dragon from harming me." the tone in her voice dampens when she mentions how he got her.

"I saw the two of you flying over us the other day. To me, the two of you seem to fly great alongside each other." I remember how the two of them were growling and roaring at each other.

They remind me of a couple having an argument, but I won't mention that right now.

Mallory guides me to her chambers which are miraculous. Her bedposts have a silking fabric hanging loosely in between them. Her sheets are an ashen color and she has random flowers in pots in several places.

"I love your room." I say in awe. She just giggles and walks over to a chest and begins searching through it.

She returns cradling something in her hands.

Holding them out in front of me she lets me look.

She holds a black chained necklace with a bright red ruby and matching earrings.

"These are beautiful Mallory." I whisper. I've never seen anything like them before.

"Of course they are, they belong to the royal family. They were once our mothers, but she left them for whenever and if Everest took a mate." She smiles.

"Are you sure I could wear them?" I ask. Baffled that she would hand something so precious over to me.

"Of course. It'll be okay. They match your gown for tonight anyway." Mallory exclaims excitedly.

I think she's even more excited about tonight than I am.

I'm anxious on how tonight will turn out.

Chapter Eleven

Everest

"**S**o you're saying that Willow's mom *was* pregnant when she married Raguel?" Winslow asks Vance in a not so believing tone.

"Yes. I knew it went against our tradition to have a child outside of the mate bond. We had plans to become mates but when Raquel threatened her clan, she made a brash decision without me." Vance growls, opening and closing his hands into fists.

"So, Willow isn't just part dragon. She's full blooded and not only that but she carries the DNA of the strongest and oldest living dragons across the continent?" I ask.

Now, everything finally pieces together. Klaudia married Raguel to save the illusive clan in the south. She was barely pregnant when she did, which is why he always abused Willow, denying her as his heir.

Vance shakes his head. His lips formed a thin line.

"The thing is Vance, she shows no kind of outward signs of being a dragon. I'm pretty certain I know why she doesn't." I recline back into my chair.

Vance looks like he's waiting for me to speak. I know the man just found out his own flesh and blood was still alive, and this may be a pretty touchy subject.

"Just know this Vance, if we had all known the truth years ago this would have never happened. But Raguel knew she wasn't his daughter, so he and his priest whipped her when she was a child. He hit her again, while I was there and I put an end to it." I talk slowly enough to watch his expression.

"And did you kill him?" He asks.

I shake my head, "No, unfortunately I couldn't start a war without my men."

Vance scoffs, "The fuck you couldn't. You didn't put an end to it unless you killed him. Your a fucking dragon, one of the strongest might I add. You could have killed him on the spot." Vance growls.

I raise my hands in an attempt to keep him calm.

"And how do you think Willow would have felt when I killed the person who she believed was her dad at the time?" I argue with him. We still haven't told Willow everything. Although I suspect she already knows.

Vance growls in frustration, running his hands through his curly hair as he paces the floor.

"She may be the exact replica of her mother, but she got the curly rats nest from you." I snicker.

He turns and gives me the 'I can kill you' look.

"What attracted you to my daughter?" He decides to ask.

I actually debated whether or not to tell him it was how she tasted but decided to refrain from that.

"She treated me like an actual man instead of like a king." I informed him. Remembering how Willow looked daydreaming at the sky with her hair waving in the wind.

"If I'd have known she was alive all these years, I wouldn't have just laid there in that damned cell." he mumbles to himself.

"Well she's here now. So we'll see if her dragon will decide to show itself, then again her dragon may just decide to sleep forever." Winslow finally decides to add his own comment.

Both Vance and I turn in unison at him.

"And why the fuck are you even here?" Vance growls approaching him.

"He's here because he loves to be nosy as shit." I mumble while flicking a pen.

"I'd like to escort Willow to the ceremony anyway, Everest. So, I should probably get ready." Vance heads to the door of my office while giving Winslow the side eye.

I nod him away and sigh.

"Just so you know, I believe women are devious when left alone together." Drake grumbles in my head and I chuckle.

He informed me this morning that he would be escorting my sister and Willow while Darcian was healing.

I didn't mind though, after the week we've had.

"So will you leave your mating mark on her tonight?" Winslow has the audacity to think I wouldn't.

Growling, I rose from my seat, "And why would you ask that?" I demand.

"Since she has never even shifted or knows anything of dragons, it could be fatal for the both of you to mate this early on?" He speculates.

Growling, I lean forward.

"The next time you have the audacity to speculate towards me or my mate, your king and queen, I will not hesitate to rip your throat out, Winslow."

Winslow hangs his head, making himself seem smaller in my presence.

"Yes my Lord." He rushes out in a quiet breath.

"You are dismissed." I wave with a hand towards my office door.

I watch him leave and wait for the faint click of the door shutting before slouching back into my chair.

With all the new information Vance has given me, we now know for a fact that Willow is a pure dragon.

However, the scars on her back tell me that Raguel knew.

He took it upon himself to have her beaten in order to make her dragon submit. Beating a young dragon can cause their dragon to go into a deep sleep, never showing itself.

Klaudia's clan, the southern clan, are an illusive clan. They prefer to stay to themselves in the mountains, claiming the summits as their homes.

I remember my father telling my sister and I that it's hard for us to even breathe in their home, due to the high elevation.

Glancing out of my window I watch the sun begin to sink, signaling that it's time for me to prepare for this evening.

Rising from my slouched position in my chair, I leave my office and head to my chambers.

Willow will be with Mallory until the ceremony begins, then she will be all mine.

Entering my chambers, all I smell is her.

That wildfire and sweet hibiscus scent tingling my nose. My cock responds instantly to her scent, throbbing in my trousers.

With a groan I readjust myself.

I quickly dress into something that I can shift easily into, the thought of having Willow beneath me only intensifies my growing desire.

A simple dark shirt and matching trousers with my boots.

I tie my white hair up until it no longer touches my neck. My hair stands out against my deeply tanned skin. My mother used to tell me that my dragon was special to control such an outward appearance.

She used to say it would mean that I was strong, able to do anything in the world. I didn't believe her then, but now as long as I had Willow beside me, I believe I could do just about anything.

"Everest, it's almost time. Mallory is going to keep Willow busy until everyone gets inside your library." Drake's voice reaches the inside of my mind.

I had wanted to surprise Willow with the library when we got here. But when everything with Zephyra happened, I waited.

Our ceremony will be held in the Kings Library. I have made it official with my council that I will be giving the entire library to Willow.

I even threatened to hand them over to Vance if they said I couldn't. Vance even made a show about how he'll kill them in their sleep if they thought his daughter wasn't worthy.

"That sounds fine. I will be down there shortly." I replied. I leave my chambers and head for the library.

The library is under the castle, our ancestors thought that it was best to have all of our documents and knowledge hidden underneath our home. In case there was ever a war or if we were invaded all we had to do was destroy our home and the library and our secrets would be safe underneath the rubble.

Willow loves to read and I'm sure she'll spend everyday in the library, from sun-up to sun-down.

I don't mind though as long as she's happy. I would attempt to give her the entire world if it is what she wanted.

Chapter Twelve

Willow

Mallory helped me dress into my new gown and the jewels she gifted me. Sitting in front of her vanity mirror, I watch as she applies make-up to my face.

We both decided a subtle look would be best for the occasion, since our mating ceremony was after my coronation.

The mating ceremony would be private, but the coronation would be held in front of a large crowd to bear witness to their queen.

I still haven't gotten used to the term of being a queen instead of a princess. I always thought I would be just a princess. But now, I'm a sovereign leader of an entire kingdom.

"Thank you for doing this." I mumble around Mallory who is applying color to my lips.

"You don't have to thank me. I'm just glad Ev has decided to take that stick out of his ass and take a mate." She scoffs.

She's told me all day about how Everest used to be against having a mate or anyone to rule beside him.

"If did have a stick up his ass, I'm glad he didn't have it there when I first met him." I laugh.

"Well, since he's gotten with you, I have to say that he's become a different person, in a good way though." She shrugs while pulling back to look at her work on my face.

"What do you think?" She asks with her head tilted.

Looking in the mirror I realize that the way she did it makes it seem like I'm not wearing makeup at all.

My lips are a pinkish nude color, there's minimal blush to my cheeks. And my eyelids have a shimmery powder on top that sparkles in the light.

"It looks amazing, thank you Mallory." I smile and reach across to hug her. She meets me halfway and I enjoy the familiar familial bond beginning to bloom inside my chest.

"It's time to go." Mallory whispers in our embrace.

Rising from my seat, I clasp my hands together in front of me. I follow Mallory out of her room and to wherever we're going.

I haven't explored this side of the castle yet, but it looks just like the rest of it does.

"Where are we going Mallory?" I ask. I'm not sure where the coronation and ceremony would be held but surely it's not under the castle.

"It's a surprise. Don't blame me, it was Everest's idea." She chuckles while grabbing a torch from its holder on the wall.

She opens a door that has a long stairway going deeper underneath the castle. She waves me forward and I follow her down.

When my eyes adjust to the darkness I see a faint light and shadows moving at the bottom of the staircase.

"Just watch your step, we don't want to ruin that dress." Mallory whispers as she turns to check on me.

I nod and continue to follow her down the stone steps.

With every step I make, my heart beats frantically out of place.

The thought of actually being a queen and to finally be Everest's mate, only caused my heart to beat faster even more.

Finally reaching the bottom of the staircase, I see a smiling Vance waiting for us.

"My Queen." he bows.

I smile at him, "I figured you'd still be harassing Everest?" I inquired with a raised brow.

"Well, I was until I told him that I would be escorting you to meet him for tonight." He stated matter of factly like he didn't just *tell* his king what he was going to do.

"Well, she's all yours now, Vance. Get her to my brother." Mallory sighs wistfully like I'm a precious letter waiting to be delivered.

Vance nods at Mallory and holds his elbow out for me.

"I thought you may not have manners for being away from civilization all these years." I chuckle and he shakes his head.

"No sweet girl, I may be old, but I have an excellent memory. And if I remember correctly, crimson was your mothers favorite color." He whispers as I loop my arm around his.

His tone is full of remorse and his eyes glaze over briefly.

"It was. I wish she was here. She spoke fondly of you to me when I was younger. She actually told me to seek you out if I ever needed help." I look down at the stone floor while we walk.

"I loved your mother, I loved you before you were even born, Willow. Your mother was graceful, but she was as wild as the mountains. I'm sure you and Everest have spoken about how both your mother and I are dragons?" He asked with a raised brow his eyes on me.

"Yes, he figures that Raguel has something to do with why I don't show any outward signs. Even if I never turn into a dragon, I'll still be happy." I smile at him.

It was true, as long as Eerest was beside me I'll always be happy. Even if our children turn into dragons and I don't, I will still be happy. Everest believes it will take something forcefully to make me shift.

Vance clears his throat and I realize we are at two large heavy oak wood doors.

"Where are we?" I ask him. He smiles at me and clears his throat again.

"It's a surprise." He whispers. A playful glint sparkling in his eyes.

He knocks on the double doors and they slowly creep open.

My eyes widen at the scene playing in front of me.

A library.

The walls and bookcases stretch for what seems like forever. The floors aren't floors but are beds of moss.

On the wall directly across from the door where I stand, splitting between two bookcases is a natural waterfall pouring out a small heavy stream of water.

The stream travels throughout the entire area. A bed of moss sits in the middle of one stream where Everest stands proudly smiling at me.

Many dragons that I haven't met or been formally introduced to are spaced on both sides of the streams of water.

My eyes burn from the tears attempting to escape my eyes. Not wanting to ruin Mallory's masterpiece I blink them away.

I step forward alongside Vance who seems to have puffed his chest out in front of everyone to seem bigger. My eyes can't leave the sight of Everest waiting for me on a bed of moss in the middle of two steady streams of water.

"When you reach the moss bed, kneel in front of Everest to begin the coronation." Vance whispers in a deathly silent voice.

At least someone knows that I don't know how dragon coronations work. My hands begin to sweat the closer I get to Everest.

"When we approach the waters edge, you'll take your shoes off and wade through to meet Everest. It's a symbol of acknowledging that no matter what happens, you know who you can turn to." Vance whispers again.

I nod subtly.

When we come to a stop near the water, I toe off my slippers and pull my dress up to my knees. I dip a toe into the water, surprised that it's unusually warm.

I walk through ankle deep water and reach Everest, who smiles as he offers me a hand, helping me out of the water and onto the moss.

I let my dress fall back down from where I had it bunched together, and then I slide onto my knees in front of him.

When I look up I notice the lusting look in his eyes and I attempt to hide a bashful smile.

"We've gathered here today to bear witness to the coronation of Princess Willow. A princess no longer, but a woman who will wear the crown of the dragons in front of nations. A woman who will live for her kingdom and king. A woman who will be the peacekeeper. A Queen of dragons." Everest's voice rings out in the library.

I spare a quick glance around us and notice that all eyes are both Everest and me.

"Do you, Willow, once the princess of the Northern Kingdoms, now the Queen of Dragons, accept the crown?" Everest asks as he looks down at me.

"I do." I smile at him.

He motions for me to stand with his hands.

When I stand, Everest turns and washes his hands in the water.

"I, King Everest of the dragons, will now anoint thee as Queen of the dragons, thus gaining your new name." He turns to me and in his hands sits a small dagger.

I watch with my spine as straight as a needle as Everest pricks his finger drawing forth droplets of blood.

Everest approaches me and places his finger on my forehead, drawing a pattern of what feels like circles.

"I now anoint thee as Queen Willow of the dragons, mate to the dragon king." Everest pulls his hand away from my forehead and barely nudges his head for me to face the other dragons.

Slowly I turn and look at all the dragons in the room. Some old and others young, some have children with them and others are pregnant.

Vance and Drake, alongside Mallory, are the first to kneel. Like a ripple in the water, the rest of the dragons follow their lead and kneel.

"Long live the Queen of the dragons!" Vance roars, which is soon followed by other chants.

A warm familiar hand rubs circles on my back, turning to look, Everest stands beside me looking at all the dragons.

Chapter Thirteen

Willow

Everest had introduced me to several dragons that were present during my coronation. Others were excited to meet me, while the rest were skittish.

"So, how does it feel to finally be Queen?" Everest asked from beside me.

"The same as before, it's just a title in my opinion. A title that comes with a lot of respect and duties to uphold." I chuckled as he guided me around several bookshelves.

Everest had given me his entire family library as a mating gift.

It was late into the night and soon the moon would be high in the sky.

"I can agree on that part." Everest inclined his head.

The anticipation of the mating sits right around the corner. Everest has explained to me that mating isn't just the conjoining of us. But a lifelong union.

He's also explained that when we mate, he'll bite me and leave his mating mark on the top of my shoulder. It had made me curious that if I was a full blooded dragon, maybe I could do the same to him.

But it was only a possibility. We still weren't sure since I couldn't even turn into a dragon.

Everest stops in his tracks and pulls me to his chest.

"I've waited long enough to claim your lips tonight my queen." He whispers as his lips meet mine in a slow dance.

His tongue teases my lips to open and allow access, which I do allow.

His tongue battles mine fiercely.

Against my abdomen, I feel how hard Everest is.

I let my hands travel down his chest and fist his hard member in slow strokes through his trousers.

He growls against my mouth, sending shivers down my back.

We begin to move until I feel the shelves of a bookcase on my back. Everest's mouth travels down my neck and to my collarbones, leaving wet kisses.

"This is in my way." Everest growls as he fists my dress and begins to rip it in two.

"If I can't be dressed then why are you?" I ask in a sultry tone.

Everest pulls away with a smirk and throws his shirt off, unbuttoning his trousers and kicking them away along with his boots.

The stoic Everest completely naked in front of me with a hard cock has me lightheaded and hazy.

"My queen gets whatever she wants." he smiles.

He returns to kissing his way down my neck and to breasts, taking a nipple in his mouth, he sucks.

He squeezes the other breast and plucks my nipple.

With a moan I arch my back, giving him more access to my breasts.

He rises and returns to my lips, still playing with my left breast as his other hand travels lower.

His fingers rub and tease my clit.

"Ev-" his hand covers my mouth before I can say his name.

"I know Willow. Turn around and show me that pretty little ass of yours?" Everest demands.

I've never even bent over in front of a man before.

With my face as hot as fire I slowly turn around. Everest places a hand between my shoulder blades, gently pushing me forward until I'm completely exposed to him.

Gripping the shelves in front of my face, I glance over my shoulder. Everest's hand continues to trail down my back bone until he squeezes the cheeks of my ass.

He steps forward while fisting his cock, teasing me by rubbing the head across my clit.

"Everest, you're teasing me." I whine.

The sound of a slap echoes around us. I wonder where it came from until a stinging sensation blooms on my rear.

Completely dumbfounded, I turn to see a grinning Everest. He pushes himself inside me to the hilt. Completely filling my insides.

With a gasping moan I grip the shelves harder.

Everest grunts as he pulls out only to thrust himself deeply inside me again.

"All I want to do is be near you Willow. To feel every inch of your skin on mine, for you to smell of me and my come everyday." Everest whispers against my ear as he lays over my back.

He loops an arm under my waist, playing with my clit, his other hand fondling my breasts and plucking my nipples.

"I want to be able to smell you all over myself any time an inconvenience arrives. Because you, Willow my queen, are the calm to my storm that I never want to lose." He licks the back of my ear, down the side of my throat.

With a hearty moan, I look into his eyes, "I want the same Everest." I gasp out in a short breath.

The feeling of him seated so far in me, rubbing that perfect spot, with him teasing my clit and nipples, has my mind in a fog.

My toes curl into the mossy floor, I'm sure I'm tearing it up. As hard as Everest is pounding into me, I'm surprised none of the books have fallen on top of us.

"Shit Willow. I want you to comeall over my cock. I want to feel you spasming beneath me as your tight little cunt milks my cock." Everest growls with his brows furrowed.

I know he's as close as I am to coming. I can feel the familiar sensation of euphoria and tingling in my limbs begin.

I don't have enough breath to even speak to him as my thighs and legs begin to shake. My breathing comes out choppy and my vision blurs.

In one swift motion Everest has me turned over facing him, laying on the bed of moss while his cock never leaves the inside of me.

I wrap my legs around his waist pulling him close to me as I wrap my hands around the back of his head. Intertwining my fingers into his hair.

With a growl Everest's mouth finds that sweet spot where my shoulder meets my neck. At first he kisses and licks.

Then in an instant, a penetrating feeling soars through me.

He's biting me. Leaving his mating mark. Marking me as his to everyone.

The pain and pleasure combine, becoming one and sending me over another ledge.

The mixture almost overwhelming, I bite into Everest's own neck to ground myself.

I feel Everest's thrusts becoming stiff until with a stiffening growl he stills.

Letting go of Everest's neck with my teeth, I lay my head back, closing my eyes.

Everest doesn't let go of my neck until our breathing slows and we become a tangled mess of sweaty, shaking, limbs.

My eyelids become heavy to hold up and my breathing feels like it's muddled.

My eyelids become too heavy and I can't hold them open anymore. I'm thrown into a form of darkness.

Chapter Fourteen

Everest

I let go of Willow's neck and look at my handiwork. The mating mark is already healing into a scar between her neck and shoulder.

"It's healing already, Willow." I informed her.

She doesn't respond so I prop myself up above her.

Her eyes are shut, and breathing is low.

Too low for even a human.

"Willow, wake up." I shake her shoulder, attempting to wake her if she were asleep.

"Damn it Willow, I need you to wake up!" I demand, yelling at her sleeping form.

She doesn't even stir or flinch.

"No, this is not happening." I growl as I scoop her into my lap, cradling her in my arms.

"Drake, help! We need help. And clothes. In the library, it's an order. And keep Vance out of here!" I yell in my head. Ordering my comrade and closest friend.

I continue to shake and beg for Willow to wake up. Footsteps eventually run up behind me and I growl defensively at whoever it is.

"Easy now, it's me. Here put this over the both of y'all." Mallory growls in a hushed tone as she throws a pair of robes at Willow and I.

Drake and Winslow appear from behind her.

"Tell us what happened?" Drake asks in a cool manner as he approaches Willow's body.

I growl and bare my teeth at him, "Do not touch her!"

He retreats immediately with his hands held up, palms facing me.

"We just completed the mating, I thought she might've fallen asleep. But she won't wake up. Her heart beat is too slow, and her breathing is too shallow." I whine as I rub my forehead to Willows.

The sound of a dragon roaring outside the library doors sets me on edge. I already know it's Vance whose number one goal is to protect Willow.

"This is what I was trying to warn you, my king." Winslow whispers with a docile tone.

The sound of breaking wood causes the three of them to turn their heads with grim looks.

"Where is my daughter!?" Vance roars stepping over the splintered wood doors.

His eyes land on me. Me holding his daughter. His daughter who isn't moving, or looks like she's not breathing.

"You." He growls. His amber eyes glowing and his dilated pupils shrinking.

"Shit." Drake curses under his breath.

"Vance. She's alive. But *you* need to calm down before anything happens." Mallory tries to reason with the angry father across the library.

"What did you do to my daughter!" Vance hisses. His lips curl, revealing all the many teeth he has.

"I did nothing to her. I gave her my mark and then this happened. You think I'm a fool to harm the woman I love?" I've yet to tell Willow I love her, but I say it in front of her father like the pleas of a dead man.

I've always known, deep down, that I love her. I just haven't voiced those words specifically.

"I should kill you." He growls, his threat is a promise.

I sigh and bring my forehead down to Willow's. Listening for signs of life.

I can't hear anything. No shallow breaths, no thready heartbeat. Nothing. I'm met with silence.

Holding back a groan, I gently rub her face and kiss her lips.

Gritting my teeth, I lay her head gently on the moss.

I turn toward Vance, "Then kill me."

Chapter Fifteen

Willow

My body feels weighed down, like something is holding me here.

It's so dark, but extraordinarily hot.

I need to get back to Everest. My mate. My kingdom.

A growling sound comes from behind me. Turning around to the sound, at first I see nothing. But then a shape starts to form.

A sleeping dragon, curled into a ball.

The dragon has a diluted gold and brown color to their scales, a slender frame with a narrow face.

Horns on either side of the top of its head with several on the top of its neck.

The dragon stirs and cracks its eyes open, a horrible whining sound echoes from it. Like it's in pain.

I go to say something but nothing comes out, the dragon's eyes are familiar. I've seen them before.

I've seen those eyes everyday when I wake up in the mornings. Those cerulean blue eyes. They belong to me.

Warmth spreads down my cheeks and I know I'm crying. Lying in front of me, is my dragon self. Something that was only a possibility that I could possess.

I walk forward and wrap my arms around the dragon's neck. The warmth and heat welcoming me.

Something cold fills my chest and I wince.

"Then kill me." Echoes a familiar voice.

Everest.

No. No. No. What's going on? I need to wake up. I need to get to Everest. I look up at the dragon and plead with every fiber of my being.

If the dragon is part of myself, it will know what I want.

I back away from the dragon holding its eyes. My own eyes screaming.

I watch as the dragon raises itself and shakes, its wings making a ruffled leathered sound.

The dragon walks to my side and lowers itself just how Everest did the day I rode him. Grabbing onto the horned spikes on its neck, I pull myself up and sit where its neck meets its back.

The dragon spreads her diluted gold and brown wings before lifting into whatever air is here. The force of it caused me to duck and lay myself against the dragon.

Cracking my eyes open, I'm met with a blinding light and what sounds like people yelling at someone.

I smell blood, dragon's fire, water, and the moss of the library where I was crowned as Queen.

"You'll die here boy." A growling voice drifts to my ears. Tracking the sound with my eyes I spot Vance's dragon inhaling air, his chest expanding.

And he's aiming at-

"No!" I shout as I raise myself quicker than I have before in my entire existence.

Before I know what I'm doing, I run past Everest in a blur and block Vance's fire with-

With wings!

Diluted gold and brown colored wings. When the heat from the fire lets up, I turn my head and face Vance. Catching my reflection in the water.

A slender snout, horns, an elongated neck and wings.

I huff a breath through my nose.

A growl rumbles around and I look for where it came from.

"Willow?" A hushed voice comes from behind me.

I turn quickly and wind up falling with my front legs crossed.

Another growl comes from somewhere and I stand, looking everywhere.

"Easy Willow. The growling is coming from you, it's okay." Everest says as he approaches me with raised hands.

"You are so beautiful." he laughs as he runs a hand down my neck.

"You look exactly like your mom." Vance mumbles, his dragon standing on the sidelines

"Do you know how to shift back?" Everest asks.

Ruffling my wings I'm certain he knows I don't know how.

I look at Winslow, Drake and Mallory who are all standing to the side, uncertain of what to do.

Everest inspect every scale on my hide until he feels pleased with himself that I'm not hurt from my new found fathers fire.

I circle myself and lay down comfortably while we wait for myself to shift back. Winslow and Vance talk to Everest about what could have happened. Or what caused me to shift suddenly.

Either way, I'm too overjoyed to pay attention to them.

Rolling on my back I wiggle myself along the ground. Rubbing the earth scented moss all over myself like a pig rolling in mud.

When it becomes clear they won't be finished talking for a while, I curl into a tight ball, my wings covering my head, and close my eyes for a nap.

Hopefully when I wake up, I will be able to shift back into my human self again. I want to hug and kiss Everest and tell him everything that happened.

"She's going to sleep. We should let her rest for a while." I hear Vance whisper to everyone.

Maybe, I was meant to be the mate of a dragon king.

Chapter Sixteen

Willow

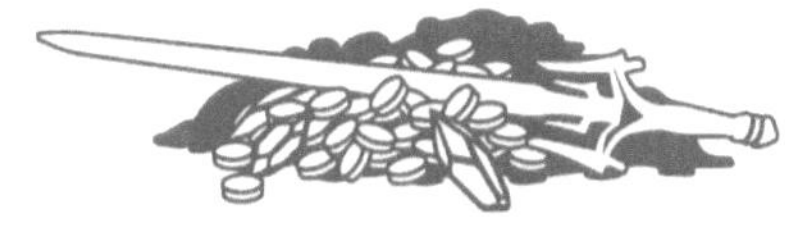

MY HEAD HAD A DULL ache that felt like it was in the back of my mind.

Groaning, I rubbed my forehead.

"Good morning, Mate." Everest's voice came from beside me.

I turned my head and squinted my eyes. Everest's white-blue eyes met mine.

"Good morning mate." My voice sounded hoarse. What did I do, yell at everyone? Suddenly the events of last night flooded my mind and I shot upright in the bed.

"Easy now. You're okay and so is everyone else." Everest rubbed my arm. I remember him offering himself up to Vance.

"If you ever, or even remotely think about offering yourself up, I will smite you!" I hissed at him with a pointed finger. Anger boiling in my veins like hot water. Anger like I've never felt before.

Everest raised his hands and sunk back into the bed.

"Yes, my Queen." He said sadly.

"But if you ever act dead on me again I will fuck you into oblivion." He shrugged.

I scoffed and swatted at his chest, "Don't be so crude Everest." I laughed at him.

He pulled me into him, "I love you Willow. Now and for forever more. If you die before me, I will most certainly follow you. Even if I'm sent to the depths of the underworld and you're sent to paradise, I will crawl my way back to you."

He cupped my cheeks and pulled me into a passionate kiss.

"I love you too, Everest." I sighed heavily and leaned into him.

Happy was an understatement with how I felt with him.

"How about we fly around our kingdom?" He offers.

I smile and nod at him, eager to explore in my new skin.

We both walk over to the balcony and Everest is the first to shift. His dragon is waiting on me.

Closing my eyes, I breath in and out until I feel something else take over.

Opening my eyes again, I see my talons below me.

A purring sound comes from Everest as I approach him and rub my side along his. Then, I bolt and jump from the balcony. My wings carry me into the sky.

Everest comes quickly to my side, flying alongside me.

Ever the man I love.

Ever the dragon who will die for me.

The man who will crawl from the depths of the underworld to kiss me.

About the author

CHARLIE ENJOYS SPENDING most of her days daydreaming about literally anything, when she's not either feeding her reptiles or chasing her son down the hallway. Living in a small town of Mississippi, although she'd much prefer being on the beach. Often mistaken as her mother's sister or carbon copy of her mom. Charlie's following in her mothers footsteps in the writing department.